LIBERATION THEOLOGY UK

BRITISH LIBERATION THEOLOGY
Edited by Chris Rowland and John Vincent

1. LIBERATION THEOLOGY UK

In Preparation

2. URBAN LIBERATION THEOLOGY

3. LIBERATION SPIRITUALITY

further volumes
under consideration

British Liberation Theology is published under the auspices of the British Liberation Theology Project, the Institute for British Liberation Theology of the Urban Theology Unit and the Las Casas Network. The Management Group of the British Liberation Theology Project is: Bishop Laurie Green, Prof. Christopher Rowland, Mr Mike Simpson, Dr John Vincent and Sister Margaret Walsh.

The annual volumes of British Liberation Theology are available on subscription or as single books. Single copies may be obtained price £7.50, p&p 50p. A subscription to all three of the first volumes (1,2 and 3) can be obtained price £20 inc. p&p. Normal discounts (35%) are available to booksellers. Quantities of 20 or over are available to other organisations at a special discount (25%) Cheques to URBAN THEOLOGY UNIT.

Address all enquiries to: URBAN THEOLOGY UNIT, 210 Abbeyfield Road, Sheffield, S4 7AZ.

LIBERATION THEOLOGY UK

Edited by
CHRIS ROWLAND
and
JOHN VINCENT

Sheffield
URBAN THEOLOGY UNIT

URBAN THEOLOGY UNIT
210 Abbeyfield Road
Sheffield
S4 7AZ

Typeset by Anne Lewis and Kathy Bhogal at the Urban Theology Unit.

Printed by Tartan Press, Attercliffe, Sheffield

4

CONTENTS

EDITORIAL NOTE

BRITISH LIBERATION THEOLOGY is the overall title for a series of Annual Volumes, designed to bring together new writing in the UK, using the methods of Liberation Theology, and recording the practice and spirituality of people involved in liberation struggles in Britain.

LIBERATION THEOLOGY UK is the first volume, and is intended to set the scene for a British Liberation Theology within the wider context of world-wide liberation theologies, and to indicate some of the ways in which liberation theology has worked and is working in contemporary thinking and discipleship. The level of the chapters in this volume is intentionally academic and pastoral. It shows how British theologies of liberation both see themselves alongside those of other continents, and also pursue distinctive indigenous agendas.

The two following volumes began at the other end - the levels specifically of pastoral and popular practice. The second volume, URBAN LIBERATION THEOLOGY, contains the stories, the theology and the spirituality of several contemporary disciples and groups, who see themselves as putting into practice or being motivated by liberation theology. They are stories of the practice of liberation in the urban scene today. The third volume, LIBERATION SPIRITUALITY, records some practice and reflection in terms of the lifestyle, discipleship, and prayer which are found among liberation-style practitioners.

The work of specific "branches" of liberation theology goes on primarily elsewhere - Feminist Theology, Black Theology, Regional Theologies, Lesbian and Gay Theologies, Womanist Theology. We have no wish to presume to "take over" the whole scene, though we do hope to have chapters or possibly volumes which reflect these growing and productive areas in which liberation theology proceeds from the stand-point of particular groups.

Indeed, it might be that our effort will encourage them also into wider publication. Of course, that would certainly not be the case for Feminist Theology, which has already created highly significant developments, and which has certainly blazed the trail both for a more general liberation theology, and also for liberation theologies from the stand-points of the women and men oppressed in other ways.

We hope at various times to include theological discussions concerning the wider theological debates in Britain, and the legitimacy or appropriateness of British liberation theologies, especially taking into account the use made of liberation theology perspectives in other contemporary British theologians. But there has been a tendency to discuss such matters in an abstract fashion - witness the endless papers, articles and chapters on the theme "What is the relevance of liberation theology to British Christians/Churches/Theology?" It may be a useful change to postpone such theoretical questions for a few years, and let some of those who want to work this way get on and see what they can produce.

We would like to invite readers to offer contributions (4,000-7,000 words). After urban liberation theology and liberation spirituality, later volumes will cover biblical theology, political theology, and practical issues in personal, community, political and public life, from liberation theology viewpoints. Please address enquiries to either of us:

CHRIS ROWLAND
Queen's College, Oxford, OX1 4AW

JOHN VINCENT
Urban Theology Unit, Sheffield, S4 7AZ

October 1995

INTRODUCTION

Since my return from my first trip to Brazil eleven years ago I was aware that my interpretative work could never be the same again. Yet I could not leave behind the theological formation of twenty years, or bid farewell to the intellectual world. That has led me on a meandering route. I sought to explore ways in which liberation theology might take root in Britain and how academic theology might contribute to many different attempts to relate experience and the Christian story in the struggle for justice up and down Britain.

But, as I have discovered over the last decade, the metaphor of "taking root" is the wrong one. Liberation theology did not need to take root, because it was in fact springing up in different places and in different forms, though with an overriding concern to understand intolerable situations which conflicted with a deep sense of what men and women might expect of one another and what the gospel seemed to demand of us all. What was required was eyes to see what was happening, and patience and humility to listen and to learn.

Although there is an admiration of "southern" theologians on the part of "northern" colleagues, there has been a certain wariness about liberation theology in the northern hemisphere. Critics often find the liberationist agenda inapplicable to the complex democracies of "the north", and find the tone too simplistic or too much infected with a philosophy alien to Christianity (Marxism). Some have even questioned whether it deserves to be called theology. And one can see why that should be the case. The characteristics of theology as it has developed over the centuries can seem abstract from ordinary life. In contrast, liberation theology in all its guises is intimately linked with human experience, which is its starting point.. Although there is certainly a method, and the contribution of Marxism as a dialogue partner, the roots of the theology in popular reflection means that it has many loose ends and is more evocative and less systematic.

9

The priority given to human experience echoes important aspects of the theology which has been so dominant over the last two hundred years. Liberation theology continues the demand that an important component of the theological enterprise is contemporary experience. It is in shanty towns, land struggles, oppressed and humiliated groups where the rebuilding of shattered lives takes place that its distinctiveness as compared with mainstream theology is most marked. The point is well made by Jon Sobrino who has for years worked in war-torn Central America. He suggests that the agenda of European theology has been more interested in thinking about and explaining the truth of faith. For liberation theologians, however, faith runs parallel to real life and is in dialectical relationship with it. The obscurities of faith are illuminated at the same time as the world's wretched condition is confronted and alleviated.

Liberation theology's over-commitment and practical involvement can make it an obvious target for criticism, for it seems to by-pass the careful questioning and necessary provisionality of much of our interpretation . For the liberation theologians the pursuit of the understanding of God comes in the midst of practice. They rightly insist that all theology in inevitably contextual and conditioned by the environment and activity in which the theologians are themselves.

An honest appreciation and analysis of where we are doing our theology is crucial. So the claim to read the biblical text simply on its own terms detached from ideology is now widely recognised as impossible. Yet "northern" theologians have been somewhat coy about their own interpretative interests, social and economic as well as ideological. The overtly committed reading from liberation theologians at least has the merit of being more clear about where it is approaching the text from, and thus posing a challenge to those of us who are more ideologically complacent.

The apparent absence of partiality in "northern" academic readings should not lead us to suppose that there may be no interest at stake. All of us involved in mainstream academic theology need to examine our consciences and ask ourselves how far our theology breathes a spirit of detachment and objectivity. There will often be struggles in the academy, but they are invariably individualised and detached from the growing gap between rich and poor throughout the world. We need to learn to be part of a community of interpretation and action in a church committed to the poor, where the concerns of the academy contribute to the challenge to the priorities of an increasingly individualistic age lacking global concern. There is nothing new in what is expected of both the church and theology. Frequently despite itself, the Christian church has for two thousand years managed to keep alive an antidote to that unfettered individualism which seeks to fragment and destroy.

There is a continuing need for a theology which reflects the dialectic between experience in contemporary Britain and a gospel which proclaims good news for the poor. Response to the poor should be a central component of our life, not an optional extra. Care for our fellow human beings should need no theological rationale, yet the lack of consensus in society as well as church demands that attention be given to this. That continues to be so in the churches, where doubts are often expressed about particular forms of the practice of charity. Whether we like it or not, Christian theology is a site of struggle. Throughout its history it has served very different ends. It can enable change, but just as easily be co-opted in the service of dominant ideology.

Enabling the liberating voice to be heard as it resonates with the lives of Christians is at the heart of the ongoing articulation of a British Liberation Theology. Reflection in the midst of the circumstances of contemporary Britain has been going on in different ways at the grassroots, mostly unrecognised by the wider church. That is beginning to change. At various consultations over the last decade (alluded to elsewhere in this journal), some of that wealth of experience has been shared, and it is our hope that their future meetings will offer an ongoing opportunity for a continuing sharing of experiences, not least with a wider audience. In the following pages there is a sample of that insight and of the different backgrounds and perspectives of people who want to identify with a liberation theology project in Britain. It is that community of interest and commitment which binds these contributions together, which were shared at the First Institute for British Liberation Theology, held at the Urban Theology Unit in Sheffield in July 1995. There, most of these chapters were heard, and much else, and we determined to commence publishing an annual volume.

Liberation theology in Britain and elsewhere is not something merely faddish and ephemeral. The words of Jon Sobrino, once more, whose colleagues and friends were murdered in El Salvador in 1989 are pertinent to our situation as we wonder whether there is really any need for a liberation theology in Britain:

"Poverty is increasing ... Oppression is not a fashion. The cries of the oppressed keep rising to heaven and ... more and more loudly...... What I ask myself is , what theology is going to do if it ignores this fundamental fact of God's creation as it is. How can a theology call

11

itself "Christian" if it by-passes the crucifixion of whole peoples and their need for resurrection, even though its books have been talking about crucifixion and resurrection for centuries? Therefore, if those doing liberation theology are not doing it well, let others do it and do it better. But someone must keep on doing it. And for the love of God, let's not call it a fashion.

While oppression lasts ... liberation theology is necessary and urgent. It is the only theology that defends the poor of the world."(1)

CHRIS ROWLAND

Some searches for "A tholeogy which reflects the dialectic between experience in contemporary Britain and a gospel which proclaims good news for the poor" is the theme of this volume. From five different contexts, five of us attempt to "get things together" in terms of Christian perspectives.

Three strands are plain. The first is the influence of third world visitors from Latin America, Africa and Asia and the issues connected with third world consciousness and politics, which has had a widespread effect on the total mood of Christianity in Britain, and in some people has produced a sense that they are about the same business but in first world terms - Christian Aid, World Development Movement, Anti-Apartheid Movement, Christian Action, Third World First and War on Want are obvious outlets for this strand, fuelled especially by CIIR and Catholic Latin American connections. The second strand is the option for the poor undertaken by some Christians in Britain, who see their discipleship and spirituality as Jesus-inspired, incarnational, "being alongside" the oppressed and deprived in personal, community and societal terms. The Catholic religious orders, the newer protestant lay communities, and the groups of people in their twenties in community houses are obvious manifestations of this. The third strand is the wider social, political and theological history of our times. This latter has sent a few of us scurrying from the neo-liberal or conservative-lurching ethos of Britain today into a search for alternative ways of looking at things and getting things together better. All these strands doubtless meet in each of us differently.

In the first Chapter, I attempt two tasks. First, I try to give some kind of. argument in favour of doing liberation theology, picking up some of its basic characteristics, and urging that they are legitimate for theology in any situation, and relevant to Britain now. The lines of a liberation theology inevitably bear the marks of its origin - and the groups in which it has been formulated. I argue that there are special reasons why liberation theology in developed forms had not yet emerged, and especially why it does not yet come from many of the poor and oppressed themselves. Consequently, liberation theology comes mainly from those who work "alongside" the poor. And even there, it has functioned as a personal and small community inspiration, rather than a social or political movement. The lines of a liberation theology from the inner city are drawn. Finally, the standpoints and contexts of others who work this way are brought in.

Christopher Rowland, exiled from his native Doncaster into Cambridge and Oxford, found Latin American liberation theology as a reversion to his own discovered radicalism of the New Testament. He asks, from long involvement with Christian Aid, why do Church people in Britain love the poor overseas, but hate the poor on the streets - and in both cases find their Christianity only supporting their prejudices? He finds the only answer in rediscovering what he elsewhere describes as "radical Christianity", which he here acknowledges as sectarian, anti-establishment, counter-cultural and alternative. He expounds Luke as a model of a missioner from the radical Jesus tradition, addressing a church all too readily "at ease with itself".

Andrew Davey illustrates how a classic liberation theology methodology works in an inner city deprived multi-racial area. He describes the physical, social, economic, political and cultural environment of a disrupted community, and finds it strangely like Leonardo Boff. Davey did his own congregational self-conscientization in Peckham, and found that his multi-racial and diverse "community of outsiders" began to resonate with the experience of the marginalised in the New Testament. Like Rowland, he finds Luke's double vision illuminating for the present divided Church, and seeks ways whereby the New Testament-like witness from Peckham can even help convert the wider church.

Chris Wiltsher takes it for granted that Christianity ought to be on the side of the oppressed. But who are the oppressed in Britain today? He makes a good case for considering the vulnerable, excluded white working class and lower middle class - Will Hutton's growing "Middle group" in his 40-30-30 society (2). Wiltsher lays the ground blocks for a liberation theology which begins there - with the demands for inclusiveness, fairness and common-interest as anglicised versions of the more heady but not often heard slogans of oppression, justice and solidarity. Certainly, a growingly divided Britain now needs to heed not only the underclass but the non-class.

13

Andrew Bradstock illustrates the continuing dialogue with developments outside Britain. From frequent visits to Nicaragua, he tells the story of events there since the fall of the Sandanistas in 1990. What does this mean, when set beside the fall of eastern communism at the same time? Certainly, it releases us from clinging on to the coat-tails of Marxism - if we ever did. But what happens to the grand design of a liberation theology actually to produce a better society? Perhaps, Bradstock says, we have to be more modest in our hopes, more realistic - but equally, more tough, more self-conscious, more separatist (!), more based on hope. And, of course, this asks whether we in Britain are not at the start of a longer march than we thought, from the days when the welfare state could be assumed, and a kingdom theology of love of neighbour was thought adequate to tackle the Powers.

We make no attempt here to systematise results or to develop whole theologies.(3) The position of origin and inspiration, and the commitment, are clear enough. The work of creating more extensive theologies comes later - though doubtless a few, like myself, are already at it.

JOHN VINCENT

Footnotes

1. Jon Sobrino SJ Companions of Jesus. The Murder and Martyrdom of the Salvadorean Jesuits. London Catholic Institute for International Relations, 1990.
2. Will Hutton, The State We're In, Jonathan Cape, 1995
3. The use of liberation theology in recent theoretical works is a welcome development - especially Stephen Pattison's Pastoral Care and Liberation Theology (1994) and Peter Scott's Theology, Ideology and Liberation (1994) in the Cambridge University Press "Studies in Ideology and Religion" series. Cf. my review, Epworth Review, Sept 1995, pp. 126-127.

JOHN VINCENT

LIBERATION THEOLOGY IN BRITAIN, 1970-1995

John Vincent is Director of the Urban Theology Unit, Director of the Institute for British Liberation Theology, and an Honorary Lecturer in Biblical Studies at Sheffield University, where he is Supervisor of the Doctoral programme in Contextual, Urban and Liberation Theologies. Recent books include <u>Radical Jesus</u>, <u>Britain in the 90's</u> and <u>Discipleship in the 90's</u>.

1. From Whom and For Whom?

In Britain today, the people who are likely to read a book like this, or any book on theology, are mainly middle class. They thus have a very deep commitment to particular self-interests in the society. Their culture is a culture of enlightenment, education, moderation, responsibility and personal compassion. Unquestionably, the residual Christian assumptions and ethic within the nation as a whole rest upon it. For the limited number of people who are within the churches or within Christian communities, this basic ethos is variously elaborated and deepened by the church's repetition of the gospel, and the debates within the Christian denominations and communities.

The middle class location of Christianity in Britain inevitably limits the hearing of the Gospel. There is a continuing "suburban captivity" of the gospel. The churches bear witness to this by the evident fact that Christian congregations in Britain are more numerous and influential in market towns, in suburban areas, and in city or academic centres, than in "urban priority areas", inner cities, city housing estates, poor country areas, urban villages and mining areas. The demographic details of this broad picture have been repeatedly set forth, and need not be repeated here. (1).

The result of this is the "take-over" of the Christian contribution by the middle class. The already clear vested interests of the middle class have become the received and accepted version of Christianity. Christianity thus supports the values of the middle class, such as the goodness and importance of the family and the family home, of established societal structures, of entrepreneurial opportunities for all, of responsible stewardship of the various elements and interests of society as a whole, and of law and order as the necessary means whereby these values can be protected and perpetuated. Elements in Christianity which are at odds with this dominant picture are disregarded. (2)

Yet, such elements, at odds with the received consensus, are a vital part of the Christian contribution. We shall describe them later. But here we must pause to observe that, on any reading whatsoever, it is always unwise for the church's contribution to be assumed to be supportive of the values of any one section of society, or to be totally evacuated of possible alternative influence within it. (3) At their best, Christians have always adopted an attitude of being

17

"in, but not of, the state", or of having a "critical solidarity" with those in power, or of being free both to say "yes" and to say "no" to the values prevalent in society. Christians do not need to be prophetic, much less liberationist, to see that this "yes, but" and "no, but yet" attitude is essential if they are to retain any authenticity - or even be of any distinctive use. (4)

All theology is, and has always been, contextual. All theology is done in the first place by listening to the questions which arise for people, and those questions are determined by their contexts. Even and especially theologies which come to us now as dogmatic were created originally within and by their contexts. (5) Human questions concern the problems or the riddles posed by existence within the place concerned. The Christian tradition is used to answer the problems and riddles posed by human existence in particular places, times and histories, and a new mutation of Christianity and Christian truth results, which is formulated into a theology.

Questions concerning the meaning of life, with which a great deal of theology is occupied, are more likely to come from cultured middle class groups than from uncultured non-working class groups. A middle aged middle class professional woman in the west of England is twice as likely to be interested in religion, or to have religious experience, as an unemployed uneducated male in South Yorkshire. (6)

It is therefore not surprising that most theology appears as irrelevant, intellectual, academic and unnecessary. It is, after all, written mainly by people who are answering the questions that come to them in their context, that of the university, the theological seminary or the church. The questioners are university or other students, or fellow teachers or members of the same guild or professional sub-group. Whether Christianity was ever intended to answer questions like theirs is never asked. It is taken for granted that it is perfectly legitimate to use the storehouse of Christianity to answer the questions which the contexts propose, provided the contexts are those where theologians are "normally" found! My conclusion is:

Tell me where you live
and I will tell you what the questions are,
for which you use theology,
to provide answers.

Or, as we have been saying at UTU for twenty years, "Where You Are is Who You Are." And we must now add: "You'll use the Gospel to answer the issues of Where You Are".

Or, if this looks too much like the theology of "answering", let us recall the trick of Paul Tillich: there is a "correlation" between the questions one addresses, and the answers one receives. (7) The conundrum is inviting: Do the questions I ask then totally determine the answers theology gives? Or do the answers theology gives totally determine the questions I ask? Such a conundrum is certainly not capable of rational solution. Hence, one has to withdraw into a theological determinism or into a natural theology, dependent on one's taste. For liberation theologians, as we know, this emerges in more developed forms as "the hermeneutical circle".

For, of course, theology is never simply contextual. Theology is created when some new elements in the context bring into immediate possibility and relevance, some elements from the biblical and historical tradition. My argument is that the present context of the realities of life in Britain today calls to the church's remembrance decisive elements in the biblical and historic Christian tradition which have always been there, but which remain dormant until they are needed.

If one asks, are these elements of the essence of Christianity? I would say, Yes. But it has taken our present plight for us to see them. Or, in the language of John's Gospel and of parts of the tradition, the Holy Spirit discerns the signs of the times and "leads the disciples into all truth". (Jn.16.13), "brings to their remembrance what Jesus has said" (Jn.14.26), or "takes of the things of Jesus and declares them to disciples" (Jn.16.14). The Spirit does not invent new things, but "takes of mine" (Jn.16.15). Just so does the divine call within the church function. (8)

The legitimacy of taking the context of the poor in Britain as a starting point for theology can only be answered by a "why not?" You must start somewhere. By what right did you assume that Christianity was legitimately to be used to solve the problems of the educated, the middle class, the university people, the academics, the enlightened despisers, the philosophers, or the religionists? If you say, "we're as much entitled to some of the goodies as you are", then fine, sit back and listen to what the Gospel says to the neglected, for once. We will discover that the whole biblical and Christian tradition, in fact is about just that.

2. Beginning with the Poor

What, then, might a theology look like which took as its location and dynamic the experience of people who have thus far not been its origin and purpose - the poor? Precisely, Liberation Theology is based upon the consciousness of oppression, and is written from the situation of the neglected, and for their sake. Let us first recall how it functions for those on the "underside" of society.

First, a liberation theology is based on a sense of the intolerable. It is not only that people are suffering, but that they are suffering improperly, unjustly, that their suffering should not be. The situation is intolerable because it is about things which ought not to be tolerated. From the common sense of human existence, from the dignity of every human being, from the long history of democracy, justice, equality and fraternity - from each arises the strong demand that oppression is not and should not be the fate of human beings anywhere. (9)

But second, also, the oppressed always live in a situation in which some are oppressed and other are not oppressed, in which some are exploited and others are exploiters. A liberation theology does not arise in a situation of commonly experienced calamity - such as a war, or a natural disaster, or a national change of fortunes, all of which in fact produce a common spirit of defiance in the face of adversity. A liberation theology does not arise as a result of what lawyers call "acts of God". Rather, it arises very much as a result of "acts of fellow human beings". The situation in which liberation theology arises is a situation of perceived and felt inequity inherent in actions and structures created by people. The oppressed and exploited live in a society in which they live beside oppressors and exploiters. Indeed, modern communications and technology ensure that the oppressed are constantly reminded that they are at the bottom of a pile which has other people at the top of it. TV, videos, computers, radio and advertisements, constantly oppress the poor with the images of the rich. The life of luxury lived by the non-poor constitutes both a cause of revolt, and a call to change, exacerbated by the unproven and mean demand that all the poor could "get on their bikes" and become non-poor if they wanted to. (10)

Beyond this, thirdly, liberation theology exists where there are hopes and aspirations that society and human life can be better. Within the human heart, there are yearnings, desires, ambitions for a life of wholeness in which anxieties and angers about basic essentials are removed, and in which human ambitions can find some fulfilment. Hope is a vital element in any situation of oppression, in which people cry for their liberation. Christian hope adds the dimension of the biblical and historical promises of God. (11)

20

These three aspects of the consciousness of oppression are common human characteristics, which for Christians among the oppressed become overlain with the Christian story and with Christian theology and hope. Basically, however, they are common human responses to the state of being oppressed. The Christian story and Christian theology simply and significantly add the dimension of God's presence with and action with the poor, epitomised in the biblical story, in Jesus Christ, and in the practical movements of Christians in history.

The invitation of a British liberation theology to contemporary Christians is this: Are there ways of acting, thinking, and working for change which are more coherent and practical under this rubric than under any other? It is a legitimate question to ask: To which human beings with unbearable burdens and pressing agendas does a theology have any promise? The question can be sharpened: Negatively, do you anywhere else hear the word which can be a word of life? Is there any other theological method or theological bag of "goodies" which offers the same or a similar invitation and opportunity? Liberation theology provides an invitation and opportunity to begin with what is burdening and oppressing you, and to work through a procedure, a praxis which can serve you. By serve you, I mean not only take with absolute seriousness the present burdens under which you labour, and not seek to spiritualise them, psychologise them, or even sociologise them, but also realistically press the points of soreness until their real character is perceived, some ruling paradigms discovered which open up new avenues for change, and some practical actions done which actually begin to transform the oppressing situation.

3. The Right Time?

Why has it taken so long for a British Liberation Theology to develop?

First, because a liberation theology has to be done on the basis of experience of a particular kind - experience, especially, of oppression. Most of those who write, read or practice theology in Britain are not themselves oppressed, or experiencing life near to the oppressed. Moreover, the few who are practising liberation theology at the base of society have very little time or energy left for writing books of theology. Liberation theology is being done in Britain in many inner city locations, by people working in housing estates, or in advice centres, unemployment drop-ins, action groups, women's groups, or in campaigns on poverty, homelessness, racism, sexism or welfare rights. Those who do so on the basis of Christian theology invariably have a few books of South American liberation theology beside them, or quote Martin

21

Luther King, or Desmond Tutu, or Allan Boesak, or Dorothee Solle, or James Cone or Rosemary Radford Ruether. Apart from that, they look for books relating to the realities of Britain today such as the writings of David Sheppard, Austin Smith, Colin Marchant or perhaps myself (12); or more secularly, those of Jeremy Seabrook, Peter Townsend, Frank Field and others.

The second reason why a British Liberation Theology has not yet been written is the obverse of the first. Those writing theology in Britain belong to a fairly closed elite of professionals who mainly quote other theologians - that is, pursue the history of doctrine. Liberation theology only comes into the syllabus as a late development, originating outside Britain, pursued mainly by Roman Catholics, and dangerously related to revolution. I recall the slowness with which Karl Barth (I write as a former student) was pursued in Britain. Precisely the same reasons I have just mentioned were given for marginalising his work - it was only "the latest fad", it originated outside Britain, it was pursued mainly by non-Anglicans and it was dangerously political. British theology is by tradition insular, moderate, banal or philosophical, depending upon your viewpoint! And, especially, British theology does not respond well or quickly to developments initiating outside this country.

A third reason for this absence of an explicit or developed British Liberation Theology is the fear that it is not appropriate. As a general criticism, this will hopefully be answered in later volumes. Part of the question about appropriateness relates to whether we are living in a situation of oppression: this is the subject of endless reports, many of them from within the churches. (13)

How far a liberation theology always in fact has arisen or must arise "from the bottom" is hard to establish from its examples in the third world. Most theology is written by and for theologians or theologically literate people - and so it is with most of the available third world liberation theologies. The point has often been made by the theologians who write liberation theology in South America or South Africa that there are at least two tasks for theology (14). First, to be alert to what is happening in history, and especially to the poor, and then to use the biblical and historical tradition to interpret it and speak prophetically on the basis of it. Second, to sit alongside the oppressed, those revealed by the analysis as the poor, and to seek to understand with them what is revealed by the tradition for their salvation. In both cases, theology is the "second act". It awaits the discernment of history, it awaits the cry of the poor, and only then goes on to speak. In both cases, also, the theologian must make a personal decision, must make "an option for the poor", must take sides, and put him/herself somewhere different as a result. (15).

Such are some of the factors that go towards the emergence or development of a liberation theology.

So it was in the case of a British Liberation Theology,. After meeting for a number of years, the British Liberation Theology Project meeting of April 1987 spent some time in analysing the various elements which are present in a third world liberation theology, and asking "what elements are already coming together in contemporary divided Britain?" We listed nine:

1. The recognition of the reality of a post-Christian situation in Britain;
2. The rising consciousness amongst women, black people, the poor, and others discriminated against;
3. The tragic loss of the Christian story to most of those now in poverty and deprivation, and the response of some to this;
4. The growth of small people's churches and communities "at the bottom" of society, which are workshops for linking bible and experience;
5. The reclaiming of the Radical tradition in the Bible;
6. The rediscovery of British radical Christian personalities, movements and groups of the past;
7. The emergence of strong, indigenous, local theologies within the inner cities and other deprived communities;
8. The use of Christian stories and symbols in the peace, anti-apartheid, ecology, development, anti-poverty and other contemporary movements
9. The agonising of the middle class and suburban churches, and the determination of some there to act.

The Consultation members identified with Jesus's declaration and programme for action, "to proclaim good news to the poor, to release those in captivity, to give sight to those who are blind, to set at liberty those who are oppressed, and to proclaim that this was the acceptable time of the Lord." (Luke 4. 18-19). The Consultation concluded:

We celebrate the places where this is already being fulfilled;
We commit ourselves to making it a reality with others;
and we invite others, inside and outside the churches, to join us in the enterprise,

as we ourselves join together in the struggles which inform and demand it.

4. From the Poor?

One decisive issue deserves special attention. A Liberation Theology arises "from the bottom", from the poor, from the disadvantaged. However, in the main, the poor in Britain are not at present the creators of a liberation theology, Why is this? Are there special reasons for it? Are there any signs even within that negative picture of elements of the "liberating practice of the poor", that is needed? Let us consider the negative factors in detail, and see why this absence is still almost complete.

1. There is little popular consciousness among the poor.
There is no "movement" of the poor. This is largely because the poor in Britain are in a minority - perhaps 15%. Also, they are invisible. They live where others do not go - in inner cities and separate council housing estates. Also, they are divided. The poor whites, the single parents, the redundant workers, the Afro-Caribbeans, the Pakistanis, let alone the disabled, the gays, the lesbians, rarely get together. And the enterprise society continually "creams off" the "best" of the poor, and turns them into entrepreneurs, (16) I omit women from this list, as they are certainly not a minority, and because they have in fact developed the consciousness of which we are speaking, at least in many sections.

The only good side to this is that although there is no common consciousness among the poor, there is certainly a common consciousness among various special groups of the poor. "The poor" in Britain are such specific groups, and we must not say they do not exist because they do not all look alike, or do not act or speak together or with a united voice. (17)

2. The poor do not use the Bible
The Bible is not used by the poor - not surprisingly. First, liberal biblical criticism, as taught in British universities and theological colleges, has largely removed confidence in using the Bible. Those who do use it are called "uncritical" or "neo-fundamentalist" (18). Secondly, the biblical stories are associated in the minds of the poor with "the enemy", with "them" - the school teachers, social workers, politicians, clergy and other professionals who appear to run the society as it is. The biblical models have been appropriated by the straight society and its functionaries.

Thirdly, the Bible and theology are learned even in poor churches as part of middle class spiritual enlightenment, or in terms of the private comfort, consolation and meaning-giving, which appear to be what the preachers call "salvation". They are not learned as the description and rationale for human liberation.

Despite all this, there are manifestations here and there of a "people's bible study". Hopefully, we shall see more of it. (19)

3. There is little popular movement for liberation.

Vaughan Jones put it in 1984: "to have a theology of liberation, it's first necessary to have a historical movement towards liberation". (20) The British poor as well as the rich have imbibed a morality of endurance, of the "stiff upper lip". Adversity is supposed to "bring out the best in people". Further, all the political parties are run by the middle class or by salaried or waged working class. This includes the Labour Party. It is both hard and unusual for the bottom 15% to join or participate in party politics, even those of the Labour Party. It costs money to pay to join, to go to meetings, or be able to offer spare time. (21)

Yet there is a movement for liberation among the ex-poor, the conscientised middle class, who are often Christians, like those with whom I work. Their struggles, often on behalf of the poor, are a real factor in Britain today. So we work from what we have got.

4. There is no specific church of the poor.

This is natural in a country where the Christian story is appropriated by the ruling powers. But it is also the result of the British denominations "hogging Christianity to themselves", so that extra or para-ecclesial Christian communities are actively discouraged or opposed. Where they occur, as in the House Church movement, they are largely middle class. I believe there is a submerged history of popular Christianity somewhere: but its relics are hardly visible today. (22)

A People's Church will emerge and flourish one day, I believe. Meantime, the denominations keep things fairly tightly clamped down, among their own members, when they can. Certainly so far as Christianity in general is concerned, the denominations discourage the genuine and indigenous popularisation of Christianity among the poor, doubtless for fear that it would be vulgarised and changed. Just such is my hope, that we will get vulgarisation and change - perhaps back to the original Christianity!

However, there are small local congregations of the poor within the present British religious denominations - and a few poor here and there within the congregations of the non-poor. And they are beginning to discover that the richer churches <u>need</u> to listen to them, as <u>Faith in the City</u> pleads.(23) Whether the richer churches will like what they hear, much less be able to do anything about it, is another matter.

So, then, a British liberation theology is "from the poor", in so far as it deals with their situation, even though they rarely do it for themselves, and it is from "alongside the poor", inasmuch as its advocates are mainly quasi middle class or ex-poor who work and live with them, not least in inner cities.(24)

The Boff brothers' book, <u>Introducing Liberation Theology</u>, makes clear that liberation theology has to take place at different levels and through different activities. They name three: (25)

1. The professional level. At this level theologians work at liberation theology as a method of doing theology, comparing it to other methods, working it out theoretically and methodistically. This level is only now beginning to happen. It had to wait until there was enough going on at the other two levels.
2. The pastoral level. Here, church pastors and priests, educated in the knowledge of Bible, tradition and pastoral practice, utilise these to promote biblical salvation and liberation among the people to support and extend the liberating activity of the people. At present in Britain, this level, I am arguing, already exists, though naturally only among certain laity and ministers, especially those whose vocations, sometimes influenced by liberation theology, are among one or other group of the poor.
3. The popular level. Here, the poor, the dispossessed, or the underclass, work for their own liberation, using as prime tools, the story of God as liberator, and developing for themselves biblical action communities, churches at the base. This level is beginning to be visible in Britain, but tarries for the reasons just given.

5. The Journey Thus Far

The beginnings of a consciousness of liberation theology were initially in the challenge of certain key writings from outside Britain. I was myself teaching in New York Theological Seminary when the impact of James Cone's <u>Black Theology and Black Power</u> (1969) first became clear. At almost the same time, the Latin American bishops of the Roman Catholic Church held a conference at Medellin, at which the "option for the poor" was urged, to help secure their liberation from oppression (1968). Gustavo Gutierrez's Theology of Liberation (1971) became available in Britain in 1974, soon to be followed by Jose Miranda's Marx and the Bible. These and other books secured in the main a highly critical response in Britain in terms of reviews and discussions. A specifically feminist liberation theology followed, with books like Letty Russell's Human Liberation in a Feminist Perspective. (26) Alistair Kee picked up many liberation theology pieces for his Political Theology "Readers" in 1974 and 1978. A group of gay writers contributed to Towards a Theology of Gay Liberation in 1976.

The earliest writings in England depended heavily on the speeches of visitors from overseas. Three conferences at which I was present were important: the Student Christian Movement Conference which produced Seeds of Liberation (1973), the Conference on World Mission consultation which produced Putting Theology to Work (1980), and the large conference of the "TTB 80's" group of the Roman Catholic Church which produced Towards a Theology for Britain in the 80's (1981). (27) At each of these, the main speakers were South American or Black North American theologians. And the main questions clearly were: What are we in Britain to understand from all this? and, What might arise in Britain if we took this seriously?

Many of us were, at that time, still uncertain about the usefulness of a specifically liberation theology orientation for Britain. Hence, the important volume, Agenda for Prophets in 1980 carried the sub-title "Towards a Political Theology for Britain". Most of its authors do not refer to liberation theology, but rather to the wider tradition and more recent work in the field of political theology.(28)

In the early 1980's, many more liberation theology books from the third world became available. British writing remained in the realm of reviews and articles. For myself, the Institute of Methodist Theological Studies held in Oxford in 1977, 1982, 1987 and 1992, with Jose Miguez Bonino, James Cone, Theodore Runyan, Elsa Tamaz, and Mercy Oduyoye gave much resource and stimulation.

The Urban Theology Unit included liberation theology in its teaching from the first Study Year in 1973. Soon, Peterborough of the Daily Telegraph had discovered us, and lampooned the "urban liberationists". The BBC quickly applied the term "liberation theologians" to us.

In 1980, I was one of those involved in the setting up of COSPEC - Christian Organisations for Social, Political and Economic Change. Between 20 and 30 organisations from SCM to Christian Action, from UTU to Christian CND, joined together to try to provide a forum and common front for radical Christianity in Britain. In 1984, it formed a British Liberation Theology Project, which met several times each year, and in the end carried out its work in the Easter theological consultations of UTU from 1985 to 1988.

From time to time, the call for a British liberation theology has been sounded in the British churches. David Jenkins, as Bishop of Durham, called for just such a development in his Hibbert Lecture of 1985. (29) Charles Elliott, somewhat similarly, has raised hopeful questions concerning a liberation theology in Britain. (30) Writings by, among others, Christopher Rowland and Mark Corner, have also traced elements in the development, and offered suggestive comments. (31) In April 1989, a weekend consultation and celebration, "British Liberation Theology" at Up Holland in Lancashire, called by Chris Rowland and myself, brought 52 practitioners. A flowering of liberation theology in many different ways and from many different sources was plain then and at the further weekends at Wistaston, Crewe, in October 1991, October 1993 - and the most recent, taking place as we go to press, in October 1995.

My own personal journey in the matter went as follows. In 1979, I first used the notion of the Base Community to interpret some elements in the "people's church" tradition in Britain, in an essay on "Basic Communities in Britain".(32) In 1981, in Starting All Over Again, I inveighed against the way in which WCC-inspired Christians in Europe seemed to be expected to do everything except the one thing which South American liberation theology invited them to do - write their own contextual theology. I even complained at the oppression of the term itself, which could prevent us from hearing what was being said through our own urban theologies. (33) An attempt to write a liberation style biblical theology on the basis of my own experience in inner city Sheffield is contained in Into the City, published in 1982. I had for a long time felt that an "Urban Theology" was more appropriate for our own situation, and have made various attempts at it (34). This line will carry forward in the future. In 1984, inspired partly by the 1982 Methodist Theological Institute at Oxford, I wrote in a chapter called "Theology from the Bottom":

"Wesley's work - and this little book also! - belong to the area of contextual theology which is done alongside the poor, along-side

God's acts of liberation in history. In that sense, Wesley and ourselves are liberation theologians." (35)

The journey of a British liberation theology has clearly been rather long and rather tentative. But its "pre-history" stage is now, I believe, at an end, as I think the future will show.

6. Alongside the Poor

British liberation theology has been happening in the cracks and crevices of the land more or less for a decade. Its practitioners are not people with much time for reading and research, much less reflection and writing. Most of those well versed in liberation theology in general, in universities or colleges or churches, do not themselves practice it, and therefore cannot and should not write about it. Most of those who are steeped in the essential elements of it, and are busy working practically on the basis of it, do not have the time or the spare energy to sit down and write systematically about it.

Very few have the good fortune which I enjoy, of being alongside the poor, of being involved in practical community and mission work in deprived areas and poor churches, on the one hand, and also involved in study and teaching in practical theology, on the other. I must admit that the two places in which I work - the Sheffield Inner City Ecumenical Mission as the community and mission commitment, and the Urban Theology Unit as the study and teaching commitment - were more or less my own creation, designed precisely to secure what to me had always been the essential mix, if one was to be Christian, let alone a theologian. Together they provide the essential co-existence and mutual play of deep, long-term engagement within a piece of "the world", and prolonged theological reflection and work there. Such, at any rate, has been my life since 1970. It is a peculiar accident of fortune that exactly that mix turns out to be the way that liberation theology has to be done. (36)

Since all liberation theology is contextual, my theology is a liberation theology based on my context. As my context is that popularised as "urban priority area", it is the context of upwards of 15 million out of Britain's 55 million population. So that it is not a specialist or restricted context - such as a university or a suburban context might be. But it is, nevertheless, also a special context. I can but speak from it as authentically as I can. If I invite others to say whether and where it fits for others, they would have to be, initially at least, those who share or have experienced life in a similar situation. Liberation theology seeks to give voice to the cries of people in a particular context who feel oppressed. The first test must be whether those sharing the oppression can identify with what is said - not necessarily in its form in this book, of course, which hardly any of them will read.

Whether that theology then creates resonances with others in quite different contexts is a secondary matter - though, of course, also of interest to the writer. Do other people's insights into the common experience of living in Britain today gain from this perspective "from the bottom"? If so, what then does that mean for the more customary points of view of theology? And is there not then already a nascent liberation theology of the middle class, which people bear witness to by their identification with a point of view of those at the other end of society?

There is also the particular cultural problem of attempting to speak on behalf of the underclass or the marginalised in Britain today. Their comparative absence means that Christian discourse is almost totally foreign to them. Faith in the City (37) states that only 0.85% of people in UPAs have any consistent membership in the Church of England. If one adds a similar percentage for Roman Catholics (which in places would be too few), and a similar 0.8% for the Free and Pentecostal churches, then one has around 2.5% of people in UPAs for whom the Christian story can be any kind of resource in terms of their own self-understanding and activity. And, as Faith in the City also points out, the few Christians we have got in UPAs have had the Christian story told to them by outsiders for so long that the possibility of their hearing it "in their own tongue" is only a distant one in most cases.

My experience of working for 39 years in inner city and city housing areas makes me cautiously hopeful that this state of affairs can be slowly remedied. If professional interpreters and do-gooders like myself learn to keep quiet long enough, and if we sit and work with people patiently enough, and if we are prepared to do nothing occasionally, and start learning from the people, then the Christian story does emerge again as the story of the poor and the marginalised, as it was in biblical and early Christian times.

And there is, even now, already an emergence of people's bible study, people's theology, and even people's church, which is beginning to produce our own "Gospel in Solentiname" (38) in Sunderland and Southall and Sheffield. Its first fruits are shared in action groups, inner city congregations, house groups, bible study groups, base community congregations, and in meetings of workers in these places, sometimes at UTU. It will need a few years before the voices are strong enough, and the stories and lessons clear enough, for them to be shared. (39)

For there is an enormous back-log to make up. One of the things for which I feel most guilty is that the story of what is Gospel for the poor and marginalised, and the biblical "plan of salvation" for them, cannot be heard at all because of people like myself, who in our best efforts cannot but speak an alienating foreign tongue. But it is not just a personal matter. The whole Christian endeavour in Britain for the last century and more is the story of successive attempts to "mission" the poor. David Sheppard's Built as a City describes the efforts, and it is not a bad story - but it is a tragic one.

The best that I can do is to write a liberation theology from a commitment alongside the poor. Hopefully, it will do something to establish the legitimacy of the operation, and also help us to interpret the cries of the poor as they come.

7. From the Inner City

My argument is that a British Liberation Theology is already taking place, and has been for some years, in specific parts of Britain.

In a Lecture in 1989, "Liberation Theology from the Inner City", I argued that we are now experiencing the elements of liberation theology in Britain. I quoted three stages popularly seen in Latin America. (40)

First, "the conviction of an oppressive situation is borne in upon a group with some theological expertise". I observed that this is witnessed to most strongly by "some of the women in our churches, who have learned what the Gospel is, and then tried to make sense of it in the situations of oppression which confront them - the oppression of women in society, and the oppression of the poor."

My conclusion was:

"So, a 'conviction of oppression' is not hard to come by, if you are a woman. And it is highly significant that the area in which liberation theology techniques have been most manifest in British theology in the last 15 years has been Feminist Theology. Interestingly, though many feminist theologians would see their work as broadly within the family of Liberation Theology, the writings and work of British Feminist Theology have not usually utilised or referred to Liberation Theology as such. Rather, it has been an instinctive flowering of theology in an area of oppression which has its own inner and outer

31

factors, and has produced its own insights and practice on the basis of women's consciousness." (41)

The second stage of Liberation Theology is that "the Christians in the poor churches become active". My observation was that there are certain characteristics emerging.

1. Separation: Poor churches have suddenly realised how separate, distinct and different they are from suburban churches. Instead of apeing suburban churches, they now celebrate their separateness. The middle class myth that "we are all in it together" is blown.

2. Self-Awareness: Poor Christians have become realistic about who they are. For instance, someone recently said to me:
   > "In some areas I am the oppressed -
   > I am a woman of low class with little money.
   > In some areas I am the oppressor -
   > I am white, I have a job and political party membership."
   Yet even her oppression, she realises, is relative. Others are more oppressive than she. So a myth of "Gospel simplicity" is blown.

3. Self-Expression: Poor churches have begun to affirm themselves as they are, regardless of their oddity and non-conformity within the presently arranged denominations. They are writing their own hymns (as in UTU's Hymns of the City), producing their own preachers, affirming their own styles. The myth of a false "catholicity" is blown.

4. Specialness: From poor churches, individual groups such as unemployed people, or unmarried parents, or black or gay people, have banded together as they see the need to act together. There is strength in finding allies. The myth of a unified, non-partisan church, such as the middle class perpetuates, is blown.

5. Bible Identification: The poor in poor churches suddenly hear things they know from their own experience, reflected back at them in the biblical stories. They discover that, according to the Bible, God is on their side. The myth of a non-political "treat everyone the same" Bible is blown.

6. Liberation Activity: The poor and the poor churches begin to get themselves together. They organise. They choose leaders. They exclude outsiders. They perceive achievable goals. They find allies. They do battle. They fail and learn from their failures. The myth of the status quo is blown. (42)

The third stage of Liberation Theology is "the re-writing of theology by the theologians and the people together".

I wrote:

"So, then, the Christian story is being performed all over again by disciples in our world today. The Christian mystery is being plumbed by men, women and children in street corner congregations, tower-block action groups, inner city black Pentecostal churches, urban area residents' groups, lesbian and gay support groups, and the faithful few survivors in neighbourhood communities.

Consequently, the poor people and the poor churches involved in all this, discover that they are the people of the Bible, that their activity is remarkably like the activities described in the Bible, and even that the God in the Bible is on their side." (43)

Such a theological re-writing happens in different ways. My own experience came from over 40 years' study of Jesus and discipleship in Mark's Gospel. Then, about 15 years ago, I realised that the activity of Jesus in Mark, and the conditions of discipleship described there, were remarkably like the action and the conditions of ourselves as Christians on the Flower Estate (an urban "garden village" wilderness), and Grimesthorpe (a terraced inner city area), two places where I minister.

Two results followed: First, that we began to read Mark as if it really was our story. Second, that I re-wrote the story of Jesus in Mark as an inner city story.

The first task has begun to show a few results, as recorded in a more recent lecture on "An Inner City Bible". (44) The second part, a re-writing of Jesus as a first century "inner city man" is already in Radical Jesus. (45)

8. From Many Witnesses

Many others in contempary Britain have their own liberation theology stories to tell, some of which will feature in future volumes of this series. A feel of their depth and quality is given each year in many places - for myself, at UTU itself or in the bi-annual Consultation and Celebration held in Wistaston, Crewe. At one stage, in one of the Consultations, we were divided into "Affinity Groups". There was one on Marginalisation, consisting of people "experiencing marginalisation in society and church because of their sex or sexuality". There was one on Racial Issues, of those "struggling against racial discrimination and articulating the black experience in Britain, or involved in inter-faith and inter-cultural dialogue with minority communities". There was one on Solidarity, for people operating out of "a theology of solidarity with the oppressed of the Third World and sharing their reading of reality and fundamental praxis". There was a group on Confronting Powers, of people "engaged in direct confrontation with oppressive structures of class, powerful economic interests, militarism, etc. in the context of politics, environmental or peace action".

The Affintity Group of which I was a member was headed Poverty and Deprivation - "those engaged in the context of urban and rural poverty, homelessness and general deprivation". After we had shared our personal concerns, and something about our own vocations, we went around the room, each one in turn sharing "What liberation theology is to me".

The responses were, I found, significant and moving. They confirmed me again in the conviction that a British liberation theology is on to something of vital importance to Christians today.

"Liberation is just a label for Gospel in the contemporary situation, where it is abominable that people are living below their potential. So, personally, I want to work with people living the Gospel fully, for the sake of the deprived." (Teacher in an urban school).

"There have been two processes I have been involved in, one from God and one from the poor. Both have changed my life. That seems to be what liberation theology is, part of the continuing struggle to make sense of things." (Minister on a housing estate.)

"I want to hold to the Kingdom values that got me into my work among the poor. The Gospel gives me tools to nail the injustices in society. We

need to be organised for it, so I welcome the label of liberation theology."
(Teacher in inner city school.)

"My project among the homeless embodies bits of Gospel values. But that also needs to have its boat rocked. We want to change the world, and we need each other to do it. That's why I am here." (Homeless Project Worker.)

"Liberation theology is about my problem with people and theology where they are always theorising about things. Liberation theology is about action, about doing things. I see the Church concerned with individuals and personal sin. Liberation theology says much of the sin is not personal but social. As a nurse I need to question the structures." (Nurse.)

"Liberation theology has given me confidence to come out from the Church structures and do some worthwhile things. I find support for my actions which I need." (Council of Churches Officer.)

"Liberation theology is something I'd never heard of before I came here. But it seems to be about the life I have been living for ten years. It's about freedom to be myself as an unemployed person just living with others." (Council house resident.)

"Liberation theology is the best label for the contemporary movement of people at all levels of society who are using the Gospel as a lever to get people out of oppressive straightjackets, and to prise open some of the potential and glory that have been imprisoned." (Inner city minister.)

There are many dimensions to liberation theology activity in Britain in 1995; but these witnesses will do for a start.

Footnotes

1.   Cf Faith in the City, Archbishop of Canterbury's Commission on Urban Priority Areas, London, Church House Publishing 1985, pp 27-46; Conrad Boerma, The Poor Side of Europe , Geneva, Risk Books, 1989; John Harvey, Bridging the Gap, Edinburgh, St Andrews Press, 1987.
2.   Cf the comments on "bettering yourself" in Faith in the City, op. cit. p101. A brilliant summary of this middle class view of Christianity was given by Margaret Thatcher in her speech to the General Assembly of the Church of Scotland, 21 May 1988.
3.   One may recall the statement of WR Inge: "The Church which marries the Spirit of the age will be left a widow in the next generation." On the

35

variety of attitudes to society in Christian history and theology, see D Forrester, Theology and Politics, Oxford, Blackwell, 1988, pp 27-56.

4. In Britain in the 90s , JJ Vincent, Methodist Publishing House, 1991, I attempt to extend current middle class values such as, fulfilment, enterprise, initiative, and wholeness, by urging A Full Life for All, Making Enterprise Common, Local Initiatives, and Celebrating Diversity.

5. R J Schreiter, Constructing Local Theologies, SCM, 1985, pp 93-98; L Green, Let's Do Theology, Mowbray, 1990, pp 16-18. On all theology as context related, cf Forrester, Theology and Politics, op. cit., pp 66.

6. So David Hay, Exploring Inner Space, Harmondsworth: Penguin, 1982, pp 118-127. Cf Vincent, Into the City, Epworth 1982, pp 116-117.

7. Paul Tillich, Systematic Theology I, Nisbet, 1953, p8. "The theology correlates questions and answers, situation and message, human existence and divine manifestation".

8. "It is the task of the Spirit to develop and realise the divine and human significance of this unique event as it affects different cultures"; to "preserve continuity" between "that time" of Jesus, and the "today" of history. Leonardo Boff, Trinity and Society, Burns and Oates, 1988, pp 193-194

9. What I here call the "sense of the intolerable" is called by C & L Boff "The perception of scandals", Introducing Liberation Theology, Tunbridge Wells, Burns & Oates, 1987, p2. Robert Graves recalls Great War experiences causing "the inward scream, the duty to run mad"., The concept of the "intolerable" is very like the New Testament "scandal". The Greek word skandalon is traditionally translated as "stumbling block", understood as "that which causes someone else to stumble", "that which is an obstacle to someone else". The "stumblings" or "obstacles" are often understood as "causing sin, or giving occasion for sin". The cross is a "scandal" in 1 Co. 1.22., 1 Cor. 1. 26-29. L Boff, Church: Charism and Power: Liberation Theology and the Institutional Church, London, SCM, 1985, p20 says the method of liberation theology "begins with indignation at the poverty experienced by God's children".

10. The suggestion that the unemployed should "get on their bikes" and go to find work was made by Norman Tebbitt, the then Secretary of State for Employment in 1986.

11. Interestingly, the otherwise critical Vatican Instruction of 1984 begins with strong affirmation of the "Aspiration" for liberation (Sections I and II).

12. See David Sheppard, Built as a City, Hodder & Stoughton, 1974; Bias to the Poor, Hodder & Stoughton, 1983; Austin Smith, Passion for the Inner City, Sheed & Ward, 1983; Journeying With God: Paradigms of

Power and Powerlessness, Sheed & Ward, 1990. Colin Marchant, Signs in the City, Hodder & Stoughton, 1985.

13. Cf. the Petition of Distress from the Cities, Urban Theology Unit, 1993. See now the stories and essays in God in the City, ed. Peter Sedgwick, Mowbray, 1995; Hilary Russell, Poverty Close to Home, Mowbray, 1995.

14. C & L Boff, Introducing Liberation Theology pp 4-9.

15. Theology as the "second act" is in R. Gutierrez, A Theology of Liberation, Maryknoll, Orbis; London, SCM; 1980, p 11; Gibellini, The Liberation Theology Debate ,SCM, 1986, p5; J. L. Segundo, The Liberation of Theology, Gill & Macmillan, 1977, pp 6-9; C and L Boff, op. cit. pp 6-9.

16. Cf Ruth Lister, The Exclusive Society, CPAG, 1990, on the exclusion of the poor from participation in democracy. See further reports from CPAG, 1-5 Bath Street, London ECN 9PY

17. For an analysis of the various groups comprising "the poor" in Britain, cf Hardship Britain: Being Poor in the 1990s, CPAG, 1992.

18. Typically, students trained in contemporary theological faculties, who arrive at UTU and find us actually using the Bible in a serious way immediately label us in this way.

19. "People's Bible Study" goes on in many small communities and groups in Britain, but is not yet recorded. Some of the best examples so far come from women's theology. See Ruth Musgrave, Believing Women: Eight Experience-based Bible Studies , Women in Theology, 1986. Cf my article "An Inner City Bible" in Using the Bible Today , ed. D. Cohn-Sherbok, Bellew Publishing, 1991, pp 121-133. Also Good News in Britain, ed. JJ Vincent, Sheffield Urban Theology Unit 1994.

20. V. Jones, What is our Theology of Liberation?, Christian Socialist Movement, 1985, p2.

21. J. Seabrook, What Went Wrong? Working People and the Ideals of the Labour Movement. Victor Gollancz, 1978.

22. Cf my essays, "Basic Communities in Britain", Putting Theology to Work, ed.. D. Winter, Conference for World Mission, 1980, pp 59-66; and "People's Church" in 2020 Vision ed.. H. Willmer, SPCK, 1992, pp 65-81. Also my Alternative Church, Belfast: Christian Journals, 1976.

23. Faith in the City, pp 100-104. See also the pamphlet Discovering Faith in the City with suggestions for churches in "comfortable Britain" (Archbishop's Commission for Urban Priority Areas, 1988); also Staying in the City: Faith in the City Ten Years On, Church House Pub, 1995.

24. This is the basic argument of my lecture, Liberation Theology from the Inner City , Edinburgh: Methodist Mission, 1989; Sheffield, Urban Theology Unit, 1992.
25. C & L Boff, Introducing Liberation Theology, pp 11-21.
26. For details of books cited, see Liberation Theology: A Documentary History, ed. L.T. Henelly, Maryknoll, Orbis 1990, pp 1-119.
27. Alistair Kee, ed., Seeds of Liberation, SCM Press, 1973; for Putting Theology to Work, see note 22; Towards a Theology for Britain in the 80's, Leeds: TTB 80's, 1981.
28. Agenda for Prophets, ed. Rex Amber and David Haslam, Bowerdean Press, 1980.
29. D. Jenkins, God, Politics and the Future, SCM, 1987, pp 105-116.
30. Charles Elliott, "Is there a Liberation Theology for the UK?", Heslington Lecture, York University, 1985.
31. Rowland and Corner, Liberating Exegesis , SPCK, 1990; Corner, "Liberation Theology for Britain", in New Blackfriars, February 1988, pp 62-71; Corner and Rowland, "Bibliography: Introduction to Liberation Theology", Modern Churchman, 1986, No4, pp 28-31.
32. See note 22 above.
33. Vincent, Starting All Over Again, Geneva, World Council of Churches, 1981, pp 13-18.
34. Vincent, Into the City, op cit; "Towards an Urban Theology", New Blackfriars , January 1983, pp 4-17; and my lecture on "Urban Theology - A Liberation/Bondage theology for Britain", at the Society for the Study of Theology" in Oxford, 1984, published as "Where You Are is Who You Are", in Grassroots, March-April 1986.
35. Vincent, OK, Let's Be Methodists, Epworth, 1982, p 69.
36. Many South American liberation theologians divide their time between parish work in the barrios for most of the year, plus writing and teaching in the Pastoral Institutes during 2-3 months.
37. Cf Faith in the City, p 33
38. I refer to E. Cardenal, The Gospel in Solentiname, Maryknoll, Orbis 1985; cf R. Sugirtharajah, Voices from the Margin, SPCK, 1990, pp 5-6 and esp.. p 434f on "the repossession of the Christian Scriptures by ordinary people".
39. Some hints are in Gospel from the Poor, UTU & Methodist Home Mission Division, 1984, and Good News in Britain. See also recent issues of City Cries (ECUM). Urban Theology Unit in 1992 started a series of booklets under the title People's Bible Studies, Vols. 1 and 2 are Ed Kessler's "Secrets of the Parables" - The Good Samaritan (1992) and Lost, Found and Overpaid (1995). Cf also Margaret Walsh, Here's

Hoping: Heath Town, Wolverhampton and the Hope Community, Urban Theology Unit, Sheffield, 1992; now in God in the City.

40. JJ Vincent, Liberation Theology from the Inner City op. cit, pp 3-4.
41. Ibid. p 6
42. Ibid. pp 7-8
43. Ibid. p9 .
44. JJ Vincent, "An Inner City Bible", see footnote 19.
45. JJ Vincent, Radical Jesus, Basingstoke, Marshall Pickering , 1986, esp. pp 11-58.

Place of Publication is London unless otherwise named.

CHRIS ROWLAND

THE GOSPEL, THE POOR AND THE CHURCHES

Christopher Rowland is Professor of New Testament
Theology in the University of Oxford. For some years he was
Chair of Christian Aid Latin America and Caribbean
Committee. He is also an Honorary Lecturer at the Urban
Theology Unit. Author of Christian Origins and Radical
Christianity, co-author of Liberating Exegesis.

1. Evidence from the Churches

For years now, Christian Aid has been supporting poor people in many parts of the Third World and has been the recipient of a fund of wisdom and insight from those poor communities. It seeks to persuade the churches, and community at large, of the priority of the responsibility to poor and needy. For a period of two years, between 1992 and 1994, I was involved with members of Christian Aid in the planning, gestation and birth of a project entitled "The Gospel, the Poor and the Churches". (1) In it, we are allowed to hear the attitudes and reactions of Christians like ourselves on every page as they seek to respond to the researchers questions. It is a rich treasury of opinion which illuminates the present state of the church and enables us to catch a glimpse of how we all view the relief of poverty.

The relief of poverty was not a major concern for all churches, and frequently was in competition with other more pressing "Christian" concerns (eg evangelism and pastoral support). Different reasons were offered for poverty in the Third World and in the UK, with a much less sympathetic attitude to the poor in the UK. The sources of information about poverty were the media rather than Christian teaching. No-one spontaneously pointed to Christian teaching as a source of their understanding. The striking visual images in the media were top of the list. Church-goers would appear to be no different from the general public in the character and source of their knowledge. Those who were best informed often had personal exposure via an overseas visit or working in a Third World country. There was little evidence of much more than a selective series of quotations from the Christian tradition and hardly any evidence of a more sophisticated theological explanation of the causes and response.

People in the Churches coped with the issue of poverty in differing ways. The evidence suggests that most church-goers are not hard-hearted. Feelings are intense, but how people deal with the feeling differs. On the one hand, there were those who expressed feelings of anger at unfairness; a desire to help; shame at the differences between rich and poor; admiration of the poor. They responded by action, believing that however small their contribution, it could help to alleviate poverty. On the other hand, were those who also expressed feelings of anger and yet the enormity of the situation led

43

them to avoid the issue or explain it away. The researchers drew the threads of the research together by outlining the different types of response:

1. Corrupt Third World governments and the poor were to blame for poverty; solutions lie in greater aid and the encouragement of greater self-reliance; by and large, poverty is a subject usually avoided.

2. Responsibility for supporting the poor lies mainly with governments and charities, rather than churches; poverty is just one of many concerns facing churches; there is a tendency to avoidance of poverty.

3. The poor are victims and deserve our charity; poverty is one among many concerns for the church.

4. Structural analysis of the social world is a necessary preliminary response which leads to advocacy of solutions for economic and political change; there should be a general Christian responsibility for the poor.

5. Structural origins for the origins of poverty are recognised; there is some responsibility of the poor in this country for their own poverty; there is a clear mandate for church involvement and a 'bias to the poor' is needed and should be a key priority for individuals and churches.

6. Structural origins of poverty are recognised and comprehensive solutions advocated; the church has a major role in such activity so there is a need for a 'bias to the poor'; poverty is no fault of the poor.

Neither social position nor denominational membership were found to be significant factors in determining the different attitudes, which are influenced by a person's world view, perception of church's mission and nature of their experience of poverty. In general, an individualist outlook on society combined with a literal approach to belief, characterises people who adopt unsympathetic or neutral stances in relation to poverty, and for whom relief of poverty has a relatively low personal priority. By contrast, a less individualistic, more corporate, outlook combined with a questioning or analytical approach to doctrine, tends to be found among people who see the need to explore the structural origins and socio-economic solutions to poverty, and for whom poverty is a central issue of concern.

This report allows us to have a glimpse of the spectrum of attitudes of the British Christians and as such offers us a general outline of the context in which we do our theology. We have before us some flesh put on the bare bones of our hunches and our anecdotal evidence. We are shown a range of views on poverty and reminded of the range of types of beliefs which are found not just in different churches but in the same church. That means we cannot go on teaching and preaching without being sensitive to the very different needs which are to be found in our midst as well as in society as a whole. What is most striking, is that there is an absence of any widespread evidence of ability either among clergy or lay people, either to offer coherent explanation of why as disciples of Christ one should want to behave in particular ways towards others, or to find this a natural resource for coping with poverty and a particular challenge to those involved in theological education.

2. The Measure of Mission

The church's task is to share in the mission of God in Christ in the power of the Spirit, but clearly there is a lack of clarity about what that should involve. We find it hard to agree on what evangelism means. Is one message a means of grace? Or is it essential to recognise that difference of personality and context demand difference and particularity in the form of the message to do all we can to enable people to hear it? This is now being recognised. In my church (the Church of England) there is a document on mission, The Measure of Mission, which starts with twelve examples of contemporary mission before reflecting on their character and drawing out the implications for a definition of mission in the light of scripture. The Measure of Mission sets out Ten Marks of Mission which arose out of its investigation of the different projects:

1. To witness to the good news of Jesus and his Kingdom.
2. To enable those called by God to become committed disciples of Jesus and members of his community.
3. To renew the church as one agent of God's concern for the world.
4. To advance in the discernment of God in the company of others.
5. To heal the sick, feed the hungry, clothe the naked, visit prisoners and show hospitality to strangers.
6. To love our neighbours as ourselves and our enemies without qualification.
7. To seek justice and peace of the kingdom and to identify and challenge the corruption of power.
8. To suffer abuse for his sake.

9. To be a sign of God's power to reconcile divided peoples
10. To enable us to be fully human after the image of Christ.

The method adopted in The Measure of Mission is very different from the Roman Catholic Church's statement on evangelisation, in the encyclical Evangelii Nuntiandii, which is more abstract and conventional in its enunciation of the church's teaching. There are drawbacks with both. The Roman document at first sight does not appear to be attentive to new situations, while the Anglican document seems to allow its theology of mission to be determined by the projects which its team chose to investigate. The Measure of Mission is seeking to start with where we are but might be in danger of allowing what the committee members thought were good examples of mission to determine how the tradition should be read, rather than allowing the tradition its full scope to offer a critique and guide. That being said, the end result in the latter is inclusive in its presentation. The 'action/reflection' model in which what we are doing is examined in the light of scripture, tradition and the tools of social analysis follows the pattern of liberation theology. The report has the advantage of seeking to be true to where we are, of dealing with the real world (which is why it's worth taking the Christian Aid report seriously) rather than offering bland statements which reach no one.

3. Mission in the Early Church and Today

There is a continuing need for a theology which reflects the dialectic between experience in contemporary Britain and yet seeks to be faithful to a Gospel where there is a preferential option for the poor and needy which pervades the ethos of earliest Christianity. The task of persuading the churches of this is central. To do this demands a careful and accurate assessment of the character of early Christian evangelisation. One important recent contribution has come from Alan Kreider who has argued that the reason the church grew in the first three centuries was not that people went out and preached the Gospel on street corners or in local debating halls. (2) Indeed, he says there is very little evidence that they did that at all, and apart from the injunctions to the immediate disciples of Jesus and Paul to evangelise, the first Christian communities do not seem to have seen it as part of their role to go out and persuade people to become Christians. Rather, evangelisation took place because there were worshipping communities distinctive, and to some extent apart, given to public demonstrations of their faith in acts of charity and if necessary in martyrdom. As a result of his study of the early church, Kreider poses very searching questions for the contemporary church:

46

"The early Christians....ask us some questions. 'At work or at home,' they might well ask us, 'are you known to your neighbours? Are you known as members of a superstition, a deviation from the norms of accepted behaviour? Are you distinctive because of Jesus whose teachings and way offer you perspectives and way of living that are new? And how about your congregations?

In the way that they function and worship, are they becoming communities of peace and freedom which are evidences of the truth of the Gospel? ..... As you prepare people for baptism, are you equipping them to live freely in the face of the addictions and compulsions of our time? Are you teaching them new narratives.... so that they are being reformed into people who are distinctively Christian? Finally, in your worship, what do your rites.....say about your churches' beliefs and priorities? Are your rites strong and living, enabling you to address the issues that really trouble your communities? Do you evaluate your worship primarily by how it makes you feel or by the extent to which it shapes your character - as communities of faith and as individual Christians - so you live like Christ?

This evocation of early Christianity is a 'sectarian' picture which sits so uncomfortably with all that we hold dear about religion, particularly in the mainline churches. (3) If it is correct, it is not surprising that many in our churches find the Bible foreign to them. That experience of being a marginal group is hardly the ethos of much white British Christianity. If, as Kreider puts it elsewhere in his article, 'joining the Christian community meant a conversion to marginality', then the gap between the ethos of the New Testament texts and 'comfortable Britain' is great. From the position of discomfort, persecution, oppression and minority status throughout history, people have found that the Bible has resonated with their lives - and that applies to all of us both rich and poor when those moments of our vulnerability strike home and we become people who suddenly find ourselves on the margins of normality. It is that sense to which liberation theology has borne witness as a voice of protest and hope against the demanding and enslaving principalities and powers of our day. (4)

4. Luke the Evangelist: Challenge to a Comfortable Church

How do we confront the difficulty that the Bible and Christian tradition of its interpretation speak of a lifestyle for strangers to a dominant culture, a way which is at odds with contemporary values? As the Christian Aid report indicates, we are part of faith communities which are in character, inclusive and often relaxed in our doctrine and attitudes. There is much to be grateful for in all of that, and the liberal part of me would never lightly leave go of something which is also very much at the heart of the Gospel. As we struggle to make sense of ourselves as Christians in continuity with the New Testament, as groups who are seeking to offer something distinctive while accepting the fact that we are caught up in the values of our age as Christians have always been, is there anywhere we can go in the New Testament? I want to suggest that there is one text in particular which begins to address the obligations of the 'comfortable Christianity' of the majority in Britain: Luke - Acts. (5)

What led Christians to write and so put their traditions on a par with the written scriptures of Judaism, of which they considered themselves to be the inheritors, remains a mystery. One of the ways whereby Christians sought to ensure its survival was through seeking to persuade (and perhaps at times placate) those in power (Theophilus may have been one such person). So part of the task of Christian textual production in its earliest phase was to position itself over against a dominant culture, whether it be a dominant form of Judaism or the ideologies of the wider Greco-Roman world. Luke (among other reasons) wrote in order to present a religion which conformed to the canons of Judaism, and would not completely exclude the penitent rich and mighty. (6)

5. Varying Purposes of Luke - Acts

Luke - Acts has been in various ways at the cutting-edge of theology in the North. First of all, as one of the synoptic Gospels, Luke and Acts have been rich resources in the quest for Christian origins. Such an interest demands a rather different approach to the text in which questions of sources move to centre stage. Secondly, Luke - Acts has been seen as the harbinger of emerging catholic Christianity. A variety of reasons have been suggested for this, some of which are touched on in this essay. Its concern with Paul cannot conceal the differences which emerge between the Paul of Acts and the one which meets us in the epistles. This can be seen as a domestication of the apostle to the gentiles into a more conciliatory figure more appropriate to a church in which consensus rather than conflict is the order of the day. Also,

Luke's concern with the whole gamut of salvation has been seen to be a retreat from the urgent expectation of primitive Christian eschatology and a response to the problem posed by the Delay of the Parousia. (7) In all of this, there is perceived to be a loss of vision and enthusiasm and the slow 'degeneration' into catholic Christianity. Such views, less prominent than once upon a time, can, with the benefit of hindsight, be seen to reflect the particular concerns of a dominant Lutheran New Testament exegesis. (8)

Thirdly, Luke's treatment of the Jews relates to the most pressing theological issue of the last fifty years: Christian theology's contribution to anti-semitism. Assessment of the contribution of Luke - Acts to this process has been variously made. (9) There is ambivalence in the texts. The hostility and suspicion, particularly marked in the Gospels (eg the harsh and uncorroborated Luke 16:14) can be matched with the ambivalent Acts 5:34ff and 23:2ff. Yet there does appear throughout both works to be a supersessionist mentality at work. Non-Christian Jews seem to be part of that recalcitrant body which has been part of the story of the people God from the very start (so Acts 7) which prompts the pessimistic quotation of Isaiah 6:9 at the close of Acts 28. The proof of Christianity as the proper fulfilment of the Jewish tradition has the effect of excluding those who fail to agree and are thus excluded from the providential action of God through the Spirit.

6. The Gospel and Culture

Luke is interested in rediscovering a lost continuity with the past. This is evident in passages which are most pertinent to my theme. Familiar passages in Luke's Gospel suggest a very different perspective from convention: the clarion-call to liberation in Luke 4:16, the insignificant Mary and Jesus' birth in obscurity in chapters 1-2; the women followers and supporters (8:2f; 13:10; 23:27; 23:49; and 55); Samaritans (10:25ff; 17:11); the concern with the 'prodigals' (15:1ff). Less explicitly linked with Scripture is the uncompromising attitude towards wealth and poverty (to which should be added the prominence of women in the narrative, though as recent commentators have pointed out, this prominence should not be overplayed). (10)

On the other hand, there are the apparent nods in the direction of accommodation with 'the mammon of unrighteousness' particularly in Acts. Ananias and Sapphira's sin is deceiving the Holy Spirit rather than refusal to share their property, perhaps a tacit move away from the practice of the earliest church in Jerusalem according to Luke. The ambiguity is even more evident in chapter 16 where the utter repudiation of Mammon and the disparagement of Dives sits uneasily with assertions about the inevitability of the use of the Mammon of unrighteousness in order to enter the heavenly places. The account of Cornelius' conversion leaves open the question of the character of life of the newly-converted Gentile soldier. This is a remarkable omission given that in the following century there was widespread doubt as to whether a Christian sign up for military service. Indeed, there is little in the Cornelius episode about the meaning of conversion (11), so different from the textual remains of early Christianity in which the cost of conversion is often stressed. For whatever reason, the moment of becoming a Christian in Acts leaves the reader with little hint of the cost of discipleship for relations with contemporary culture. This suggests to me that Acts at least was intended for external consumption (and to that extent is probably unique among the New Testament and contemporary Christian texts). The focus of the story is on the evangelising of Cornelius and his companions and not the character of life of the newly-converted Gentile soldier.

Early Christianity, like Second Temple Judaism, had an ambivalent relationship with culture. Even when its adherents found themselves in positions of influence, there remained a reserve towards contemporary political arrangements which, however widespread assimilation may have been, prevented them from being readily assimilated into the Roman imperium. The early Christian communities were distinctive counter-cultural groups which sat at a tangent to contemporary culture. (12) Pre-Nicene Christianity was a dissident network of groups which owed allegiance to another king (cf John 18:36 & 19:15) and another set of values. The limits of compromise are clear in early baptismal texts like the Apostolic Tradition attributed to Hippolytus, which actually excludes those in military service as appropriate for Catechumens. Whether this applied to Cornelius we are left in the dark. Deliberately so? And for apologetic purposes? We should resist seeking to resolve these tensions which may well have been necessitated by the enduring convictions about the demands of eschatological existence in Christ in the old aeon dominated as it was by an overarching political and economic order which had still not passed away.

7. Luke's Alternative Story

The story Luke tells is remarkable in its subordination of the rulers of the contemporary world to a Jewish Messiah and a minority, dissident movement, within Judaism. The populace of Galilee is confronted with good news which differed markedly from the propaganda of the imperial world. So, despite its conventional history, Luke's Gospel hardly exhibits an unambiguous attitude towards established institutions and beliefs. It is after all Luke which portrays Jesus as predicting the destruction of city and Temple because of its inability to understand what led to its peace. In Luke, the message to the rich is not a very palatable one. The reader of the Gospel is left in little doubt about the appropriate response to those like Lazarus. The chapters after the infancy narratives have plausibly been seen as a contrast to more militant sentiments earlier in the Gospel. Of course, this may have suited the apologetic aim of a writer who wished to portray a pacific religion. But elsewhere there is little evidence of any sycophantic attitude towards Rome. Certainly, it is less obvious than in the contemporary writings of Flavius Josephus. As is well known, he became a courtier at the imperial court of the Flavians after switching sides in the First Revolt and predicting that ancient Jewish oracles spoke of the ascendency of Vespasian.

Luke is not lacking in passages which concern the poor and outcast, but in its understanding of the presence of Christ it lacks that radical edge of Matthew's vision of the Last Judgement (Matthew 25:31ff, assuming as I do that Christ's brethren are all the hungry, thirsty, naked and imprisoned). Evident elsewhere is Luke's growing concern with a church which might not be entirely poor. In Luke's version of the command to true greatness, Mark's "whoever would be great among you will be your servant" has become "let the greatest among you become the youngest and the one who rules as one who serves", suggesting that Luke's community has within it distinguished people for whom such advice has become a pressing reality. Truly, it is an injunction to opt for the poor but a reflection of a Christian community which is altogether more cosmopolitan. (13)

The focus of interest in Luke's work is the story of Christ. All else is incidental to that dominant concern. But that christological perspective includes the orientation of Christ in the Gospel towards the outcasts and rejects. In the process of convincing Theophilus of his version of the story of Jesus, Luke set the story in the midst of genres which largely were the prerogative of those who served the interests of the politically and economically powerful. Luke falls into the category of a book which seeks to set down a story which might hardly merit a record in the annals of the ancient world and, in so doing, includes a glimpse of those poor and insignificant people who were the beneficiaries of the Gospel. He does not, by any means, present a story of Jesus who merely represents the opinions of the groups of people he (Luke) may have been writing for. So, it is hardly surprising that frequently basic ecclesial communities in the contemporary world have found in reading Luke, something of that challenge and a voice which in some way expresses their own aspirations and hopes.

Luke's Gospel does not exhibit an unambiguous attitude towards established institutions and beliefs. It is after all Luke which portrays Jesus as predicting the destruction of city and Temple because of its inability to understand what led to its peace. In Luke, the message to the rich is not a very palatable one. The reader of the Gospel is left in little doubt about the appropriate response to those like Lazarus. There is little evidence of any obsequious attitude towards the dominant power of the day: Rome. Certainly, it is less obvious than in Luke's contemporary, the Jewish historian Josephus. At first sight, Luke in Acts seems to portray Rome in a favourable light (eg Acts' positive treatment of Roman officials), but there is something unusual about the portrait. What we have is the history of an insignificant person in a tiny province of the Roman empire, being made the central part of human history and the focal point of the story. Instead of that story being brought into line with Roman history, we find in Acts Rome and its representatives are related to it. The appearance of governors and proconsul and soldiers is fitted into the narrative of God's purposes focussed in the life of one who brought good news to the poor and outcasts. Cornelius' conversion and the centurion's confession are moments when representatives of Rome, albeit, in Cornelius' case, one sympathetic to the Jewish religion, bow the knee before Christ - to paraphrase the words of Phil. 2:9ff, which have in my view rightly been seen as a political statement about the lordship of Christ.

Discussions of Luke - Acts have tended to see them as attempts to play down the political significance of Christianity, by presenting the movement as non-threatening to the Empire. But Luke's writings offer an alternative vision of society which is never seen to threaten Rome explicitly, but the emphasis on the inclusion of the marginal and the reversal of status indicate that, however much Luke wanted to commend the religion as a justifiable part of the Roman world, its awkward and challenging parts had to be owned and could never be smoothed away. While there is no suggestion that Luke - Acts espouses a revolution against Rome, Christianity was left, as Kreider reminds us, in a position of non-conformity with contemporary culture, which was so characteristic of the Christian church in the pre-Constantinian era. Luke - Acts was written to churches which were relatively affluent, had tasted of the good news of justification by faith and life in the Spirit, and needed to be reminded that there was more to faith than mere religion. And most important of all, Luke wanted them to take seriously "the option for the poor".

An option for the poor is evident. In the activity of Paul, we find a story of enormous dedication and energy consisting of two parts. Firstly, there is the community formation in which groups of Jews and pagans were created, nurtured on the basis of reading the Bible in the light of Jesus Christ. Secondly, there is the task which occupied the last years of Paul's career: the collection for the poor in Jerusalem. (14) The innovatory character of the project and the effort involved in organising a collection which then had to be taken hundreds of miles should not be lost sight of. The collection for the poor in Jerusalem has few obvious parallels in the ancient world. Its prosaic nature renders it of lesser importance in discussions of Pauline theology. Yet closer examination reveals the centrality of this activity for Paul's theology. (15) Not only does he justify it christologically: "though Christ was rich yet, for our sake, he became poor" (2 Cor. 8:9). But also he speaks of it as an act of grace (8:7). The collection was to be a channel of divine aid which was both a means of alleviating misery and also a demonstration of God's character. He speaks of it in terms which are reserved elsewhere in the Pauline Corpus for the proclamation of the Gospel itself (9:12. Cf Col 1:24). The collection is part of a list of secondary items to be discussed under the heading of Paul's theology. Here is a basis for a common practice in the church. When the right hand of fellowship could be exchanged only after hard bargaining and conflict (Gal 2:9), in the matter of relief of poverty there was immediate agreement on an issue of central importance for the nascent church (2:10).

In a Britain whose goal it is "to be at ease with itself" (to quote the words of our present Prime Minister), Luke's Gospel, which may have arisen within a situation where conversion to Christianity involved a challenge to the "philosophy of being at ease with oneself", offers a timely message. Christian memory could not allow an ideal of the Christian ethos which disregarded the poor and needy. Another horizon was needed, and here, in the Gospels and the Pauline epistles, the memory of a Christ who opted for the poor is kept alive as is the need to follow in his footsteps.

Footnotes:

1. The Gospel, the Poor and the Churches published by Christian Aid in May 1994 and available from them at PO Box 100, London, SE1 7RT
2. A Kreider, "Worship and Evangelism in Pre-Christendom", Vox Evangelica 24 (1994) pp7ff
3. See also W Meeks, The Origins of Christian Morality, New Haven 1993
4. See the important study by Walter Wink, Engaging the Powers, Minneapolis, Fortress, 1992

5. See further P Esler, Community and Gospel in Luke-Acts, Cambridge 1988; C Rowland, Christian Origins, London 1985
6. See further P Esler, Community and Gospel in Luke-Acts, op. cit.
7. See the classic study of H Conzelmann, The Theology of Saint Luke, .London 1961
8. Eg E Kasemann, "Paul and Early Catholicism" in New Testament Questions of Today, London 1969 and further D Way, The Lordship of Christ, Oxford 1991
9. See J Jervell, Luke and the People of God, Minneapolis 1972 and J T Sanders, The Jews in Luke-Acts, London 1987
10. "Even as this Gospel highlights women as included among the followers of Jesus, subjects of his teaching and objects of his healing, it deftly portrays them as models of subordinate service, excluded from the power centre of the movement and from significant responsibilities" (J Schaberg in The Women's Bible Commentary, Ed C Newsom and S Ringe, London 1992)
11. See further B R Gaventa, From Darkness to Light: Aspects of Conversion in the New Testament, Philadelphia Fortress 1986
12. W Meeks, The Origins of Christian Morality, op. cit.
13. See K Wengst, Pax Romana and the Peace of Jesus Christ, London 1987
14. See D Georgi, Remembering the Poor, The History of Paul's Collection for Jerusalam, Nashville 1992
15. This is well brought out in F Young and D Ford , Meaning and Truth in 2 Corinthians, London 1990

Note: This is an abbreviated version of a lecture given at the Third Periodic Consultation of the General Synod and Voluntary Bodies of the Church of England in April 1995.

ANDREW DAVEY

BEING CHURCH AS POLITICAL PRAXIS

Andrew Davey is Vicar of St Luke's Church of England, North Peckham, London. His theological background includes years at UTU, Sheffield and Tamil Nadu, S India.

... the church of the poor is a structural channel for the coming into being of the true church ... the Spirit manifests itself in the poor and .. they are therefore structural channels for finding the truth of the church and the direction and content of its mission ... the poor in the church are the structural source that assures the church of being really the agent of truth and justice. In the final analysis, I am speaking of what Jesus refers to in Matthew 25 as the place where the Lord is to be found.(1)

Jon Sobrino S.J.

The only thing that is really new is to accept day by day the gift of the Spirit, who makes us love - in our concrete options to build a true human fellowship, in our historical initiatives to subvert an order of injustice - with the fullness with which Christ loved us. (2)

Gustavo Gutierrez

Despite some interest in the mid-eighties inner city churches in England remain marginalised and under resourced. The mainstream churches have failed to break their paternalism and develop a theology and strategy through which the essential role of the church of the poor in the whole church can be realised. This paper seeks to explore the reality of a church among the poor in inner London. After describing our context and some issues raised by recent trends and Liberation Theology, I want to explore some of the directions which congregations in marginalised communities might take in their struggle to be faithful to the word as they discern it and explore some of the Biblical hints of a theology to underpin this.

1. Context

Our church is situated in the midst of four massive deck access estates. It is a constantly disrupted community where the physical environment owes much to the blitz and the slum clearance of the post-war era and where the population contains a diversity of social and ethnic groupings. The estates suffer from a high turnover and a negative caricaturing. The estates are often the target of new government initiatives, (HAT, Task Force, local management, a City Challenge bid and now Single Regeneration Budget), often initiatives half heartedly followed by a council which realises that a far from perfect scheme is the only way to bring any money into the area.

Added to the physical environment are the socio-economic pressures (3) that people are under. Unemployment and low-paid, part-time work lead to a lack of self-esteem and stress, particularly for those with families. The everyday attempts to maintain a fairly mundane level of survival is apparent in the many pressures facing refugees, students, those with mental health problems, single parents attempting to return to work or education, senior citizens, etc. There is also what the caricature of Peckham calls "dumping" whereby many who are socially insecure (refugees, former homeless and those with mental health problems) find themselves in "hard to let" accommodation with little statutory support. Politicians do little to help. Paddy Ashdown sensationalised the situation in an *Evening Standard* article and subsequent book which did nothing to enhance the area's self-esteem:

> ... the council has dumped here, among the bewildered elderly whites and West Indians who have lived here all their lives, Nigerians, Somalis, Vietnamese, each resentful of the most recent arrivals, each mutually suspicious, each living in an island of their own. For a little extra misery, they have added the mentally handicapped (sic), cleaned out from institutions under "care in the community". There are no resources to support them, so they wander the corridors and alleys like lost souls in hell. (4)

Local clergy and councillors wrote to Mr Ashdown with a very different understanding of the community and how problems were being redressed.

The ethnic diversity of the area is important to the sense of belonging for which many long. For them Peckham is familiar territory with shops, churches and schools which give some sense of security, though for many there is a culture of fear. Particularly with a lack of personal transport (over 70% of households were without access to a car in 1991) dark nights can be intimidating. The estates stand within sight of the office blocks of the City of London and Docklands, yet the only connections are the informal early morning cleaning work which many take on to top up meagre state benefits. North Peckham is a very compact area, geographically sandwiched between areas which are potential breeding grounds for the far-right. People are often reluctant to move even a few streets into other housing areas where there is a threat of racist violence.

With most of one's energy used in keeping one's self together and a little bit of neighbourliness, there is little surplus for involvement in community or tenants' groups. The lack of organisation and management skills in the community puts pressure on professionals working in the area particularly in respect of fund raising, servicing committees and negotiating with outside bodies. A local community policeman contradicts the myths:

Don't let anyone tell you these people are scum. They are mostly very decent people trying to do their best in very difficult conditions.(5)

In the midst of all this is St Luke's. Not the only Christian community in the area but maybe the most visible through its 1950's neo-byzantine basilica. Peckham is an area where the incidence of religious observance is high. A proliferation of black-led churches as well as a network of mainstream evangelical churches echo Peckham's reputation as a place of dissent in former centuries. St Luke's through the divine lottery of the Anglican parochial system has the responsibility for a parish where 99.4% of residents live in purpose built flats. Following the 1991 census publication, St Luke's found itself top of the Southwark Diocese UPA parish listing by a massive 12 points.(6)

So what does being church entail in such an area? How can we be good news as we take on the experience of marginalisation, rootlessness, poverty, violence etc?

2. Temptations of the Urban Church

Looking at the life of churches in inner London one is aware of the need for a relevant congregational life that begins to address the experiences of the Christian community. The temptation too often is to concentrate efforts on single issues and modes of being through which the church can become side-tracked from its task of actually being church.

The leading temptation is that of the project culture. We are ten years on from *Faith in the City*, a report that spoke of the need for new styles of church. The initiative which came to dominate however was that of the Church Urban Fund (CUF), a major funding source for projects in UPAs. Though much of the CUF project work is important and needs to be applauded, it has led to a social project based culture within UPA churches. The report's recommendation concerning the fund was that it "should strengthen the Church's presence and promote the Christian witness in urban priority areas."(7) Ten years on the popular image of the UPA parish is primarily in terms of social and community work. Only recently has it been recognised (8) that more reflection needs to be done concerning the state of congregational life in UPA parishes, (both with and without projects), struggling to maintain their own life, worship and witness. It has been noted that parishes set amidst the worst social deprivation often lack the means to plan, resource or manage the type of project which CUF has promoted. Here projects are definitely out of the question as the little energy available is put into "keeping the show on the road" week after week.

Faith in the City did contain some important insights into this process, but these, for the most part, have been eclipsed by the project culture. The future of UPA congregations such as St Luke's does not depend on the development of welfare resources but on the building up of confidence and new patterns of discipleship among those who are determined that faith should be seen in practice in our inner cities.

The challenge ten years after the *Faith in the City* report is for the church to listen, comprehend, and to speak the truth of the UPA experience whilst prioritising its resources to maintain a "lively" presence. Although CUF style projects are a vital witness of Christian concern they should not be treated as the standard by which the life of UPA congregations are judged. It would be a scandal if *Faith in the City's* contribution to UPA mission is only understood solely in terms of projects, which are often short term solutions to the absence of local service provision and make a disproportionate demand on time and effort of those who set them up, particularly in terms of fund-raising and management.

The *Hope in the City?* report warns about the inertia that can set in within the project culture when an obsession with certain types of action can be the excuse for a lack of reflection and evaluation. Such an absence of critical analysis can be an excuse for not facing up to the long term problems of a community or a church. Projects have been known to dominate parish life with a litany of problems: falsely raising the expectations of UPA people, giving the church an increasingly "amateur" reputation among voluntary organisations in respect of employment practices, and disappointing client groups when funding fails or the project comes to an end and an inadequate exit plan executed. If the church is to survive in the most deprived parishes, resources need to made available for local people to be empowered within congregations and deaneries. The sustainability of marginal congregations through localised training and networking can give a future to the maintenance of an authentic Christian presence. That will be demonstrated through presence and involvement in the life, concerns and voluntary organisations of the parish community.

3. Learning from Elsewhere

Faith in the City spoke of Liberation Theology as an example which:

.....opens up the possibility that new priorities, as well as new methods, can restore to us a theology that is truly relevant to the needs and aspirations of people today.(9)

Although Liberation Theology is a third world movement, pockets of the type of social phenomena which have been its breeding ground are apparent in places such as inner London. In 1988, Leonardo Boff listed the common phenomena which suggest that Liberation Theology will be relevant to such contexts:

Social/economic conditions - poverty in stark contrast with wealth enjoyed by other citizens, underemployment, poor health care, marginalisation of population in society - particularly immigrants, refugees etc, racism, poor status of women;

Political conditions - weakness of institutions, lack of representation, over-riding of human and social rights;

Cultural conditions - poor education standards, lack of participation in national life, little recognition of cultural life of immigrant groups;

Religious conditions - churches depend on the centre for resources of personnel and funds, and the proliferation of fundamentalist sects in which those who feel forsaken take refuge.(10)

In Peckham, any theological work needs to be based in the reality of life of those living in such conditions. On a church level, Latin America has presented the challenge of the Base Ecclesial Communities (BEC). These have forced church leaders to take seriously questions of power, culture and ministry, particularly the dilemma about how poor congregations are serviced by those from a different cultural and social background. The nurture of a local vision of leadership and of self-sufficiency calls for new models of mature and self-confident churches to emerge truly rooted in the community they seek to serve. Understanding the economic causes of alienation and disempowerment is vital if the whole human condition is to be addressed.

I can remember as a theological student, being presented with the essay question - 'Is Liberation Theology naive?' We are sometimes left wondering whether it was in the first stage of its academic analysis and use of Marx, or naive in its emphasis on folk culture and the old patterns of community interdependence in the face of the onslaught of a very different mass culture from the northern continent, typified in the rise of neopentecostalism. Commentators are often dismissive of first world attempts to "do" Liberation Theology. I suspect that those of us who work under some of the conditions described earlier in Boff's common indicators, would prefer to describe ourselves as *learning from* rather than *doing* something which carries the label Liberation Theology. Similarly, the BEC experience is a very particular one, the BEC usually acts as a cell of a larger community and has developed in some areas into a mass movement. Despite the interest, the BEC model has not transplanted to the first world context where the privatised mass media culture is already well established. My reaction to books about experiments in BEC in Europe and North America is increasingly sceptical. These experiments are very self-conscious and always one off. There is little sense of the mass movement which we encounter in the writings coming out of Latin America fifteen years ago. I suspect that BEC sociological profiles may have more in common with the neo-catecumenate cells or restoration churches, examples of which we find on our doorstep.

In Peckham, I have been working with a congregation which, while learning from the struggles and insights of the BECs, is seeking its own mode of being church in its own particular context. Ched Myers' recent book contains some words of warning. First world Christians looking toward a liberationist approach need to be wary as to their assumptions and motivation:

> ....theologies of liberation claim to be reflection on practice, and mere commentary on someone else's practice deftly side-steps the question of our own. Even if we sympathise with the theologies of liberation, we are in constant danger of expropriating their rhetoric without engaging their methods. A mid-week Bible study group in our local parish does not become a "base community" just because it is so renamed, nor are we in solidarity with the poor simply by declaring we are. This is why liberation theologians have become more insistent that we who claim to understand and concur with their basic assertions

must discern our own context, respond with our own practice and reflect critically on that. (11)

In our congregation Liberation Theology has provided an invaluable methodology. Echoing Gutierrez' description of doing theology as 'critical reflection on Christian praxis in the light of the Word' (12) social analysis has played its part alongside Bible study in understanding some of the pressures and dynamics facing the area and the church. In the context of a series of such studies, we analysed how power was held in the church and society and identified the ways in which interest groups create ideology to secure their position. From there we constructed our alternative futures in the form of manifestos - manifestos which incorporated participants' insights from work with refugees, schools, political parties and credit unions.

The three manifestos that were brought to the session each approached the task from a different angle. The first was concerned with the problems of Peckham and the changes needed locally and nationally to bring about a better society. The second was concerned with how the church must change. The third tried to rewrite Isaiah 61: 1-2 and Luke 4: 18-19 as the good news for now.

Three important elements emerged in each manifesto:

1. freedom from fear, freedom from discrimination, equal shares and dignity, 'give children back their childhood', get rid of loan sharks.
2. a radical shift in relationships. The Church of England must listen to the poor, it must work to empower the poor, it must share resources for the good of the poorer parishes.
3. good news for those who do not know peace, possibility for the hopeless, freedom for those who cling to rules and regulations, and 'to rattle the conscience of those who are comfortable'.

We talked about how our faith helps us discover new possibilities and dream alternative futures. We thought about the sermon we heard on Easter Day, preached by a friend of mine from East Berlin. She contrasted the bad news of the soldiers, bribed by the authorities to say reality was no different, that the disciples had moved the body, and the good news of the women, who claimed nothing would ever be the same again. We thought about how becoming part of St Luke's changed the way people lived and thought - discovering and developing skills, confidence etc. We decided to put up the manifestos in church and ask people to look at them at Pentecost. The St Luke's congregation was felt to be an important place to create an alternative way of organising a church as we continued to equip ourselves in ways that might begin to work on making those manifestos a reality. A greater determination to participate and influence things in groups already offering the possibility of change and doing things was felt to be important.

The process enabled some of those involved to articulate experiences of social exclusion as an important stage in self understanding and valuing people whose stories remain untold and voices unheard. An important element in the process has been attempting to start where the participants are in terms of social location as well as faith and intellectual understanding. This involves taking seriously instinctive religiosity, particularly among older members, which is often not articulated, and also encouraging the discovery of the liberative strands in their stories and those of their biblical inheritance. The British theologian, Andrew Kirk, who spent twelve years teaching in Latin America encourages English UPA Christians to learn from the Latin American experience 'in the task of reflecting theologically from where they are' in the process of relating scripture and experience.(13) Like Sobrino he looks forward to:

....the church *of* the poor. No longer does the church come in from outside, as it were, as well defined body to act on behalf of the poor. They now hear for themselves the good news of Jesus and the Kingdom and seek to translate it into action within their fellowship and beyond in the community.(14)

The formation of such a church is the task we set for ourselves at St Luke's.

4. Towards a Theology of Belonging and Community

Social and geographical dislocation is a common experience in Peckham. Those who make up our church congregation have few roots in the area - only two families have any history in the area of more than one generation. Most have family roots in the Caribbean or Africa.(15) There are also local communities which our worshipping community does not draw from, notably Vietnamese and Somali. The rural poor of the third world have become the concrete-bound dispossessed of the first. That dispossession is not just the experience of poverty and limited social access, but also the stigmatising of our area and the constant experience of pollution as from traffic etc.

Walter Brueggemann when reflecting on OT land theologies wrote - '....a sense of place is a primary category of faith....'(16) Space becomes place only when there are stories and hopes lodged there. The experience of exile and captivity is the experience of coerced space in contrast with trusted place.

The central problem is not emancipation but *rootage*, not meaning but *belonging*, not separation from community but *location* within it.....(17)

The strategy for a sustainable, relevant Christian presence among the rootless and dispossessed is the struggle for a community that embraces the fight against captivity and landlessness. These elements have featured in the ongoing process of group work and my own reflection alongside the congregation.

Themes of migration, the search for 'home' and of being an outsider feature regularly in our experience and discussions.

Most of us were brought up with Bible maps which plotted in huge squiggles Abraham's wanderings through the ancient near east. On one occasion a group plotted alongside such a map their own journeys - from the Caribbean to the Southern States at the height of segregation, from London to Nigeria and back again, from rural Ulster to urban Belfast and then on to London, from the Caribbean to Southport to Balham to Peckham. All roads somehow lead to Peckham, at least in these stories!

Within those stories, we heard of the search for Christian community, of risks taken, of expectations raised and misunderstandings. The community which Abraham and Sarah drew around them seems a paradigm of our experience and aspirations, a place where blessings are shared, strangers are welcomed, faith is passed on, hope takes root, alongside faith being tested to the extreme. A community where people are drawn from traditional cultures has many hazards and pitfalls. It can also have the feeling of a counter culture apparent particularly when welcoming and hospitality are discussed. Our reflection has also helped with a partnership being created with an evangelical agency working with refugees and speakers of other languages based on our premises.

5. A Community of Outsiders

In our discussions it became increasingly noticeable that those taking part often considered themselves to be on the periphery of institutions,

65

communities and society in general. We spent time looking at how people become outsiders and how those who are insiders maintain control. In this process we used examples from the Gospels, people's own experiences, and the well-known example of the apartheid system in South Africa.

The geographical location, the encounters and the teaching of Jesus in the synoptic Gospels all point to the marginal as key to the coming and presence of the Kingdom of God. On one occasion, we took the three stories of 'children of Abraham' from Luke's Gospel (18) which all point to a concern to include those who, for whatever reason, are denied full participation in the society to which they rightfully belong. Among the marginal, Jesus discovers faith, an honesty to admit to their deficiencies and needs (19), alongside acute insight into the reality of what makes them marginal. They are the most receptive not only to the message but also to the invitation to create an alternative way of community life, on the periphery, which challenges the hegemony which others wittingly and unwittingly maintain. It is Jesus' practice of 'open commensality' not his parables of the great feast that provokes the severest opposition (20). This and other symbolic acts (not least at the symbolic level of ritual ideas about impurity) are in essence political action. Such political action is appropriate in a context where the majority of the population are excluded from any type of structural political participation. This approach of the political, which I suspect is a key paradigm for our church life in Peckham, is described in a recent article by Chris Rowland:

'By *political* in this context I mean their relationship to conventional patterns of human interaction and organisation, whether formal (like a Sanhedrin or local body of elders) or informal and traditional (like widely established practises). The political challenge posed by Jesus involved departures from norms of behaviour, status, attitude and access to social intercourse which are typical of a particular society.' (21)

The marginalised experience and understand the reality of their situation in a vitally different way from others. From the margins they perceive two realities (or narratives). First, their own immediate reality within which they must struggle for survival and look after their own as best they can. Second, from the margin they also need to understand the systems and language of insiders because it is from there that their own position is determined and the rules of that order are made. Insiders do not need the perspective of those on the periphery because their powerful situation gets them all they need. Jesus attempts to create an inclusive community for those united by suffering and their experience of exclusion. Within that community they experience the possibility of healing and hope. Jesus reinterprets the powerful's world view with outsiders in mind: they shall possess the Kingdom, inherit the earth, receive consolation - this is 'the story of marginality.....retold as entitlement'. (22) This is the starting point of the marginalised's new identity from where lives can be reconstructed. The Jesus community, and the Kingdom that is glimpsed through it, are paradigms of the restructuring of attitudes and systems which are condemned by the very existence of outsiders. There the marginalised come to understand that there can be no security in becoming an insider. Security is to be found in their growing sense of dependence on God and interdependence with each other (23) from which even the most harrowing suffering can be endured. Insiders, that is the rich and powerful, might be called to repent and join this community. It would have been this call to adopt a radical egalitarianism stance which presented the greatest challenge to the readers of the Gospel in Hellenistic culture.

It is not only in the descriptions of the early church in Acts that we encounter the first Christians attempting to deal with social division and scandal. From the discourse of the Gospel writers and the letters of Paul, we glimpse a church striving to come to terms with its memory of radical relationships. In its new cultural milieu this memory clashes with traditional notions of honour and shame (24), and the patronage and reciprocity of the new city elites (25). As new communities they were striving for a common identity. Mary Ann Beavis suggests that it is a particularly Lukan contribution to Christian ethics to combine prophetic ideas of welfare with a critique of the rich in the call for a discipleship of equals:

'.....he forges beyond the condemnation of the elite to a vision of a community of spiritual equals in which social disparities are vigorously and conscientiously addressed.' (26)

The communities of the first century were, like the inner London congregations of today, heterogeneous assortments of peoples attempting to bond and create a sustainable community life, often against a background of misunderstanding and hostility. Were the diverse and scattered early Christian communities 'good news' for the poor and insecure who formed them? In his epistles, Paul challenges those who are attempting to structure the emergent communities along the standards and norms of the society they lived in. In Corinth, the assembly consists primarily of those from the lower and slave classes. Sergio Rostagno argues that the inclusion of the heathen poor is Paul 'intuitively' realising 'the Gospel event of the last becoming first'.(27) Michel Clevenot similarly describes how Paul uses the term *ecclesia* as designating not

'....only a gathering but rather the specific practice of these communities articulated at the economic, political and ideological levels as faith, hope and love.'

and goes on to conclude from this, that:

'Our ecclesia would be therefore the place of a messianic practice in the absence of the body of Jesus, which is signified by this very practice.' (28)

The excitement of the early church was that something new was happening among the urban landless poor of the Roman Empire. Though in political terms they were powerless, there was a discovery of a bond and a vision greater than those which dominated their culture and society. Young and Ford describe the experiences thus:

'The Gospel is a proclamation of events and their central character, its transmission generates new events of suffering, conflict, foundation of communities, generosity, praise, prayer, and much else; and there is urgency about its communication which is powerfully productive of new history.' (29)

Rostagno puts the demand of materialist interpretation and a praxis-orientated faith clearly, (speaking in a fashion which demonstrates how a modern reader might respond from within his or her given context and pretexts):

'we modern Christian are in no way bound by the model for life and the social relationships practised in the Pauline community; their praxis....is an attempt at Christian life for which they have full responsibility until the day of judgement; we are not responsible for it, nor should we have any notion of blaming them for their attitude to women or slaves. We are, however, responsible for our own practice, and we are completely responsible for it.' (30)

6. *Ecclesia* as Political Praxis

So, how do the members of our church define themselves as a church community? Again we are faced with the question of the nature of the Christian community. Ethical practice does not always mark members of the congregation out from their neighbours. Peckham is, by inner city standards, a place of high religious observance as people search for meaning, identity and security in the face of uncertainty, anonymity and danger. Rediscovering the personal narrative and that of the Christian community gives expression to the values and hopes that the individual is attempting to live out and the story(ies) they find themselves part of. Christian memory 'that mediates and operates in ways that heal, redeem and transform' (31). The Christian community is a place where those values (the Kingdom) may (should) be remembered, glimpsed and participated in, and the place where the future of those stories is anticipated and prepared for.

Within the St Luke's community, there is a security in being able to function at our own speed and in our own way, but it would be wrong however to pretend that we are totally self-sufficient. We rely on the rest of the church to finance our professional ministry and to resource some of our training etc. We need our relationship with the rest of the church to be seen in the light of the radical memory of the marginalised community. Our presence within the wider church needs to be nurtured as one of vitality. To repeat Jon Sobrino, the church needs the poor "as structural channels for finding the truth of the church and the direction and context of its mission".(32) As a marginal congregation, we need to establish our 'story of entitlement' within the church through networking and using the resources available for empowerment. In some aspects our liturgy and practice will seem mainstream or traditional, but the presence of a predominantly black congregation from a range of ethnic origins is a political witness to the possibility of such a community despite the attempts of the sociologists, media and planners to write off the possibility of community in Peckham. A similar witness is vital in the wider context as the Church of England begins to realise the need to nurture local black leadership using training resources which build on their identity and experience. The catholicity of the church is dependent on the local resources and experiences of groups and congregations such as St Luke's being valued as an essential part of the church which can be vital in its redefining itself for the present in the light of the radical memory of scripture.

In the congregation at St Luke's and its parish community we find what could be described as a 'collision of narratives' as people, from a variety of ethnic backgrounds, attempt to define themselves in a context very different from those in which their personal and cultural narratives have been formed. For many, the strong narratives of fundamentalist and Pentecostal churches provide some security in response to their disorientation. The task the historic churches need to take seriously is not to substitute people's narratives but to provide a means by which a diversity of narratives may be held within a single community so that each can enrich the other. Our attempts to establish a representative ministry team at St Luke's may also reflect the need for that diversity to be reflected in the pastoral oversight of the congregation.

New approaches to scripture have affirmed the retelling of stories in the search for a relevant congregational life. Within the activity of Bible reading, we have had the privilege of witnessing people engaging in their own stories alongside the narrative of scripture in a new creative way. This has raised people's expectation of scripture as well as enriching the corporate life of the church and its strategic thinking. More work is needed on how scripture is read in a diverse community. New readings so far have emerged from marginalised groups which tend to share within themselves a common experience, eg Felder's African American Churches or Cardenal's Solentiname community. The greater diversity within congregations may create a less uniform approach to scripture. Similarly, ways must be discovered by which those narratives and discoveries can be shared and owned through liturgy and reflection on scripture in public worship.

It is noticeable that members of St Luke's do employ a 'hermeneutic of suspicion' when dealing with communications from the diocese or other levels of the church. This, I suspect, comes from that need of the marginalised to understand and work in two realities. Within the narrative of the church there is a subnarrative of the oppression and discrimination aimed at those outside the ruling hegemony, simultaneously there is a strong tradition there of those at the margins discovering liberation through corporate and individual discipleship. As our direction was discerned and implemented, especially during the Bible studies, people would readily question whether what was being presented really reflected reality as they experienced it - in society, in Peckham or in the church. Discussion about power revealed how marginality leads to suspicion being one of the few weapons in the armoury of people in their struggling for full personhood. Clergy often expect parishioners to take their 'expertise' on trust. Neutrality and the notion of objectivity need to be analysed in the light of an understanding of ideology and power. It could be instructive to ask what role suspicion takes when marginalised people encounter the tabloid press. Similarly, being wary of the leaven of scribes and pharisees is a basic necessity when responding to some attempts by the institutional church to show solidarity.

7. Implications for Ministry

Any Christian theology of ministry and mission which draws on images of servanthood, with the inevitable inbuilt inability to understand or handle power needs to be treated with great suspicion. The difficulties for African American Christians of biblical images of servanthood and slavery have recently been highlighted by Renita Weems and Clarice Martin (33). Images of service may be appropriate for those who are more used to being served (34). But those who experience marginalisation on a daily basis may be less willing to take on such a notion of ministry. Could this be one reason for those members of the black community, who are able to 'make it' academically or professionally, rejecting ordained ministry as a career option?(35) In UPA parishes the danger is often that the minister is too often seen and used as the self-designated servant choosing a role and philosophy of ministry which does not lead to participation or to enabling others and which does not always speak the whole truth. There is the danger of clergy being unable to admit to the actual power they have or becoming ineffectual because of an unwillingness to use their actual power in challenging domination.

'Whereas Jesus moved from and through powerlessness to effective power, Christians have embraced powerlessness and abandoned the vision of transforming it into power.' (36)

Models of the church and its ministry must come out of a shared notion of working for the common good as a disciple group of equals which challenges hierarchical domination. Liberation style approaches hint at the potential of action-based models where marginalised people's innate suspicion is harnessed in their empowerment.

The tasks are far from complete in Peckham. We continue to increase our awareness of the forces and structures we must struggle with in both church and local context. As confidence and insight grow, a more rigorous critique may be developed. In the meanwhile, we are aware that our presence and struggles, our actual practice of being church, must act as a critique of those forces and structures. A church which is not rooted in such a grass roots presence cannot develop a prophetic voice with credibility in marginalised communities or in the society which marginalises them.

Footnotes:

1. Jon Sobrino, The True Church and the Poor, SCM Press, London, 1985, p95
2. Gustavo Gutierrez, A Theology of Liberation - History, Politics and Salvation, Revised Version, SCM Press, London, 1988, p174
3. 1991 census returns for the council ward indicate that 15.6% of households are headed by single parents, 57% of children live in non-earning households, 10.8% live in households where there is 'limiting long term illness, 17% of households are in unsuitable accommodation.
4. 'Paddy goes to Peckham', Evening Standard, (London), Monday 8th March 1993.
5. Quoted in Alice Coleman, Utopia on Trial - Vision and Reality in Planned Housing, 2nd Edition, Hilary Shipman, London, 1990, p92
6. Based on 1991 census returns. Indicators included unsuitable accommodation, unemployment, access to personal transport etc
7. Faith in the City, CHP, London, 1985, p165 & 363
8. Richard Farnell et al, Hope in the City? - The Local Impact of the Church Urban Fund, CRESR, Sheffield, 1994
9. Faith in the City, p64
10. Based on the indices of underdevelopment in Leonardo Boff, "What are Third World Theologies?" in L Boff & V Elizondo (Eds), Theologies of the Third World - Convergences and Differences, Concilium 199, T&T Clark, Nijmegen/Edinburgh, 1988, p3f
11. Ched Myers, Who will Roll away the Stone? Discipleship Queries for First World Christians, Orbis, Maryknoll, 1994, p20
12. Gustavo Gutierrez, A Theology of Liberation, Revised Version, p11
13. Andrew Kirk, 'Liberation Theology and Local Theologies' in Anthony Harvey (ed) Theology in the City - A Theological Response to Faith in the City, SPCK, London, 1989, p24
14. Ibid. p26
15. The ethnic origins of members on the 1995 electoral roll were 61.5% West African, 24% Caribbean, 9% other African, Asian, Greek etc
16. Walter Brueggemann, The Land - Place as Gift, Promise and Challenge in Biblical Faith, SPCK, London, 1977, p4
17. Ibid. p187
18. ie the woman in the synagogue, Zaccheus, Lazarus in Abraham's bosom.
19. Maybe the New English Bible rendering of the first beatitude 'Blessed are those who know their need of God...' isn't that far from the point.

20. John Dominic Crossan, Jesus: A Revolutionary Biography, Harper Collins, San Francisco, 1994, p69

21. Christopher Rowland, 'Reflections on the Politics of the Gospels' in RS Barbour (ed), The Kingdom of God and Human Society, T&T Clark, Edinburgh, 1993, p240

22. This phrase is used by Walter Brueggemann referring to Joshua's speech at Shechem. See Biblical Perspectives on Evangelism: Living in a Three-Storied Universe, Abingdon Press, Nashville, 1993, p61

23. J Kopas, 'Outsiders in the Gospel: Marginality as a Source of Knowledge' in The Way, London 1993, p117

24. Crossan, Jesus, p70

25. "Their life centred on a meal that served as a means of integration, not just of Jews and non-Jews, but also of members from various status groups and social positions. The ethos of the meal represented a break with the city ideals of patronage, benefactions, and the quest for honour. It is not unthinkable that such criticism of city ideals could also have been aimed at community members from the 'elite periphery'." Halvor Moxnes, 'The Social Context of Luke's Community' in Interpretation, Richmond, October 1994, XLVIII/4, p387

26. Mary Ann Beavis, 'Expecting Nothing in Return: Luke's Picture of the Marginalised' in Interpretation, Richmond, October 1994, XLVIII/4, p365

27. Sergio Rostagno, Essays on the New Testament - A 'Materialist' Approach, WSCF, Geneva, Undated, p36

28. Michel Clevenot, Materialist Approaches to the Bible, Orbis, Maryknoll, 1985, pp127-8

29. Frances Young and David Ford, Meaning and Truth in 2 Corinthians, SPCK, London, 1988, p240

30. Rostagno, Essays on the New Testament, p50

31. Walter Brueggemann, The Bible and Post-Modern Imagination, SCM Press, London, 1993, p27

32. Sobrino, True Church and the Poor, p95

33. See Renita Weems, 'Reading Her Way....' and Clarice J Martin, 'The Haustafeln (Household Codes) in African American Biblical Interpretation: "Free Slaves" and "Subordinate Women", in Cain Hope Felder (ed) Stony the Road we Trod, Augsberg Fortress, Minneapolis, 1991

34. Ted Harrison in his portrait of the Church of England, Members Only, DLT London, 1994, recalls a recent hymn poll where the new

hymn *Servant King* figured highly among clergy and nowhere in
the laity's choice.

35. It is early days yet to know if the experience of women, ordained to
the Anglican priesthood, will shed any light on this or their own
problems over the lack of role models.

36. Jay MacLeod, Community Organising, p10

Note: The process described in sections 3 and 4 was engaged in as part
of a Ministry Project undertaken through the Master of Ministry
programme of the Urban Theology Unit.

CHRIS WILTSHER

ANGLICISING LIBERATION THEOLOGY

Chris Wiltsher is a Lecturer in Religious Studies in the Division of Adult Continuing Education in Sheffield University, and Warden of the Hurst House Adult Education Centre, Chesterfield.

1. Introduction

One of the clearest aspects of liberation theology is the insistence on contextualisation. Liberation theology, we are told, arises within specific contexts and is adapted to those contexts. While the general approach and spirit of liberation theology may be transferable, ideas, elements, applications must firmly be grounded in a particular local situation.

Despite this injunction, attempts to transfer liberation theology to European contexts, or to create liberation theologies for Europeans, have assumed that certain concepts are universal and transferable. One of the aims of this paper is to challenge that assumption. My claim is that at least some concepts central to liberation theology in its original South American context do not transfer easily into an English context. If this claim has any substance, the search for a British theology of liberation will involve us finding equivalent concepts for the British context and exploring what kind of theological and biblical mileage they have.

I have already introduced a distinction which is important for this paper in mentioning both an English context and a British theology of liberation. The United Kingdom of Great Britain and Northern Ireland contains four distinct countries, and many more distinct regions. In spite of the best efforts of some politicians, I am not persuaded that there is sufficient uniformity between the regions to make it easy to speak of a "British" context, at least in aspects relevant to a theology of liberation. All too frequently, in theology as well as in politics, the word British is used when what is being referred to is a small segment of the United Kingdom or its population, usually centred on London or one of the other major cities. There is more to Britain than that!

Not only is the United Kingdom geographically diverse, it also contains many distinct population groups, from those whose families have been in their particular place for centuries to those who are recent arrivals. All are British (again, despite the efforts of some), but they are very different, so different that I wonder whether a truly contextual theology can possibly speak to all of them.

Since I am, by nature and training, one who searches for unifying themes and universal ideas, I should like to see a truly British theology of liberation;

77

but the contextual issues outlined above suggest that this is an occasion to start small and grow. In other words, a British theology of liberation, if such be possible, will grow out of the search for theologies of liberation arising in the context of particular groups within Britain.

My contribution to the search will focus on the English working class and lower middle class, and in particular on members of those classes outside the urban jungles of our great cities. I am interested in a theology of liberation for the lower segments of Middle England.

It is important here to be quite clear about what I mean by "the English working class and lower middle class". For the purposes of this paper, I mean anyone who grew up in England amongst working class and lower middle class people and who has remained within that culture. A person's origins do not matter; what matters for my purpose is the imbibing of a set of values, attitudes and activities, almost unconsciously and uncritically.

In focussing on this group, I am making something of a virtue of necessity: I am English, rather than, say, Scots or Welsh, and I come from and have spent much of my life amongst members of these classes outside the large cities. However, I also think this is a significant and interesting group for proponents of liberation theology in Britain. It is a large group, but largely a silent group, not as newsworthy as some other groups, not as instantly recognisable as some ethnic groups, not as obviously in need of liberation as some groups, not as easily accessible to the national media as some urban groups, and certainly not at all responsive to the blandishments of theologians of any stamp. It is also a group which challenges many of the attitudes and assumptions of nice theological liberals, for often members of the English working and lower middle class appear prejudiced, even bigoted, blinkered, narrow-minded and self-centred, with no interest in anything outside an unhealthy lifestyle, sport and hearing about the latest sex sensation. As with most caricatures, there is some truth in this picture, sufficient to unnerve a high-minded idealist or a liberation theologian.

So this is the group that is my concern, warts and all. My claim is that for this group, the central liberation theology concepts of oppression, justice and solidarity have no significance, and must be replaced if we are to find a theology of liberation for this context. I suggest the replacement of oppression by exclusion; justice by fairness; and solidarity by common interest. Whether, having made these substitutions, we can still find a biblically grounded theology of liberation is a question to which I shall turn at the end of the paper. First, we must explore the case for the conceptual

78

changes I have suggested. Are these three concepts insignificant for the English working class and lower middle class? Are my suggested replacements of greater significance? Can the replacements do the job required?

2. Oppression and Exclusion

Liberation theology speaks to the oppressed: the marginalised, the down-trodden, the very poor. Liberation theology arises in part as a response to oppression, a means of creating and sustaining hope in hopeless situations, a channel of empowerment, a catalyst for change. Liberation theology is concerned with liberation from oppression of all kinds. But what is oppression, and who are the oppressed?

To be oppressed is to be kept subject by coercion. The coercion might be the unsubtle force of arms, military or police; it might be the financial coercion of wage slavery or overwhelming debt; it might be the religious coercion of eternal damnation. In many cases of oppression, there will be a combination of forms of coercion, each reinforcing the other to add to the burden. Whatever its specific form, coercion is characterised by apparently irresistible pressure, constantly applied, which penetrates and affects every area of life, and against which the oppressed have no weapon.

If that is oppression, the English working class and lower middle class are not oppressed. Many of them are unemployed, and most of those who are in employment earn below average wages and have little or no job security. Some are badly housed, while others struggle with mortgage debts or rising rents. Most live a relatively hand-to-mouth existence, with a week to week horizon, robbing Peter to pay Paul and lacking financial resources when things go wrong. None of them has chosen to live in this fashion. Their circumstances have been forced on them by the accidents of birth, the vagaries of fortune and the ineptitude, indifference or hostility of governments, employers, officials and their self-styled social superiors.

But they are not oppressed. They have a vote and live in a country in which the ballot result is respected. By and large, they are left alone by the police, and they do not have soldiers threatening them. They are bullied by employers and officials, but hardly coerced, and they have a variety of ways of thumbing their noses at authority, literally and metaphorically. They have access to education, to books, newspapers and a television service which is not overtly or totally controlled by the state, so that they have access to information, the opportunity to form opinions and the opportunity to express

79

their opinions. however abhorrent. Crucially, they can retreat into their own premises and go about their own lawful business without direct interference, and can even appeal to the law for protection. They are not oppressed.

They are not oppressed, but they are excluded. They are excluded from secure and satisfying employment because they lack skills and qualifications, or they have a police record, or they have family commitments. They are excluded from many of the economic benefits of society because they do not have enough money to take holidays, run cars, visit leisure centres and the like: and their few pleasures, such as drink or a smoke are condemned as unhealthy and taxed heavily. They are excluded from good education because governments will not provide the necessary resources and they do not have the money to buy education. Similarly, they are excluded from the best health care, because that is the preserve of the rich. They are largely excluded from the upward mobility of the housing market and they are certainly excluded from worries over the performance of their investment portfolios.

Excluded from so much, in general they cannot break into the magic circles, because access is controlled by those inside. A few representatives of the excluded are allowed in, to become tokens of the masses, but the general exclusivity works very well. And it hurts. It breeds frustration and anger and it wastes the talents and lives of human beings. Those who suffer such exclusion need liberation.

The liberation they need is a liberation from exclusion, not oppression. The liberation they seek is an opening of doors into the circles of privilege, an inclusion of the outsiders in the privileges - but not liberation through doing away with privilege! Those who have moved from the outside to the inside are often most vociferous in defence of their new status, which raises questions of justice and solidarity.

3. Justice and Fairness

Justice is one of those concepts which is very hard to pin down, and it becomes even harder to define clearly when used in liberation theology. Justice is not the same as equality, of any kind, yet there is an element of equality in the concept of justice. Justice is not the same as maintenance of rights, yet there is an element in the concept of justice which makes no sense without the assertion and defence of human or natural rights. Justice is not entirely concerned with order, and especially not with law and order, yet the concept of justice relies in some way on the idea of an ordering of society. Justice is, in short, a philosopher's paradise!

As so often in such cases of contested concepts, it is much easier to define the negative and to give examples of injustice. We all know when we have suffered injustice, even when we cannot quite articulate clearly what the injustice is. And, of course, for many people harsh injustice is simply a fact of life.

So it is for the English working class and lower middle class. There is no doubt that they suffer from injustice, nor any doubt that they know they suffer from injustice. But you will not often hear them saying: "That's unjust". You will hear them saying: "That's unfair!". And the difference between unjust and unfair is significant for a theology of liberation.

At first sight the difference between unjust and unfair is small. Many people would regard the two words as almost interchangeable. However, for people steeped in the culture of lower Middle England, the difference between justice and fairness is not simply a matter of words, and is not small. The key is that justice is to do with law, fairness is to do with people. Since the law is regarded as always biased in favour of the rich and powerful and against the excluded, justice is for those who can afford it. The rest of us have to put up with injustice from the system, and can do so by simply staying clear of authority as much as we can. However, we can not stay clear of our neighbours, friends or employers, and in our dealings with them, fairness is required.

This is not to say that fairness is an attribute only of personal relationships. Fairness is desirable in all spheres, even in dealing with authority. However, it is not expected that "the system" will be fair in its dealings with us, unless it is compelled to do so; and because "they" treat us unfairly, it is fair for "us" to cheat "them" whenever we can get away with it. It is not fair for us to cheat each other.

So what is fairness? Like justice, it is difficult to define, but you know when you have been treated unfairly. One important component of fairness is treatment according to circumstances: in dealing with a situation, you have regard not to absolute universal laws, but to particular local applications of general principles. I use the word principles deliberately, for these are not statements of the kind "you must...." or even "you must not....". Necessarily, fairness is not the same as impartiality, yet there is an element of avoiding partiality, in that partial treatment has to be based on the recipient's needs or circumstances rather than on relationships.

An important part of fairness is some very loose and vague notion of the way things ought to be, a notion that is handed down from generation to generation in an unspoken and largely unreflective manner - hence in part my insistence that the groups I am concerned with are defined by their imbibed culture. This notion of how things should be is not only vague, it is often very narrow, having arisen in a particular set of circumstances and undergone little challenge. Consequently, the notion which underpins fairness may be at odds with ideas of order which underpin the concept of justice. This is one reason why working class and lower middle class groups have developed their own very effective extra-legal ways of dealing with those who offend against their communal codes: the justice system does not always produce fairness, and people think they can do better.

Missing from the notion of fairness is the idea of rights. Of course, the language of rights is as common in Middle England as elsewhere, but it is part of the learned way of dealing with authority, of playing the powerful at their own game. Amongst themselves, working class and lower middle class people do not talk of rights, and neither do they look to the law to defend their rights. They do talk of entitlement, they know very clearly what they can and cannot do, and who can or cannot gainsay them, and they are very sure of their position in law: but their entitlements are part of their heritage, dependent solely on being born in a particular family or a particular group. Working class folk and their lower middle class counterparts are every bit as conscious of inheritance as any member of the landed aristocracy.

Liberation theology has grown up in a different setting, imbued with the language of rights which grew out of the Enlightenment and took root in continental Europe. There are many connections between the language of rights and the English talk of entitlements, but the connections should not blind us to the different conceptual basis on which the ideas stand, nor to the very different ways of claiming one's dues.

The consequence of all this is that a liberation theology which calls for justice will not reach the roots and hearts of the English working class and lower middle class. Calls for justice are too closely associated with long folk memories of manipulation by the powerful, and talk of rights is suspiciously foreign. Talk instead of fairness and you might touch a chord which unites.

4. Solidarity and Common Interest

Solidarity is essential to a theology of liberation. Solidarity makes it possible for the oppressed to resist coercion; solidarity allows them to unite, to emphasise, to share, to build a sense of community. Those who are in solidarity with one another are united by more than a shared interest, or even a common purpose. They have a common experience and a common commitment, to each other and to their group, and a willingness to suffer individually and collectively for the perceived good of the group.

None of that applies to the English working class or lower middle class. They are not very interested in community. They will unite in pursuit of a common interest - but only as long as it suits them, as many a trade union activist or campaigner has discovered. They have some common experience, but are more concerned to let you know of their own individual slant on that experience. They are very wary of commitment to any group other than their own kin, and will not generally put themselves to suffering for others.

At this point the myth-makers should rise in protest. For there are many myths about the English working and lower middle classes in their English rural hamlets and their grimy industrial villages. Everyone "knows" that people in such places have a very strong sense of community, that they are very neighbourly, that they resent and close ranks against outsiders, and that they suffer together.

However, for all the attraction of this picture of community and even solidarity, I fear it is a myth. The strong sense of "community" and neighbourliness rarely extends far beyond one's immediate family, and altruism is acceptable only so long as it costs little. Neighbourliness is often indistinguishable from nosiness, and much of the close knowing of each other so celebrated by some community historians is a by-product of living so close together in thin-walled houses that privacy is impossible.

Privacy is a key concept here. I have not met anyone from any kind of village background, rural or industrial, who has not bemoaned their lack of privacy. There seems to be something deep in the culture of lower Middle England which insists that a person is entitled to privacy, to secrecy, to the opportunity to do things without onlookers or overlookers. The demand for privacy is shown very clearly in the territorial instincts of the English, the desire to have a place, preferably separated from others' places, to which one can retire and within which one is unchallenged. There is a very deeply entrenched belief that what goes on in an English home is the business only of those who dwell there.

Interestingly, hand-in-hand with this insistence on privacy goes a strong sense of public accountability. You can do what you like in private, as long as you do not affect your neighbours. As soon as your private actions begin to have public consequences, or are in some way brought into the public domain, you become accountable to your peers. There is a real edge to the old crack that in England the greatest crime is getting caught.

I do not pretend for a moment that I think it is possible to make such a simple division between the public and the private, or that I accept the idea of actions which have no consequences for others. My claim is rather that, whether or not I agree with them, these notions of privacy and public accountability are part of the mental furniture of the English working class and lower middle class, and affect their response to calls for commitment or group solidarity. To be committed in the way of true community is to come out from your protective walls and open your place of security to others: the English prefer to talk over the garden fence.

This does not mean that you cannot unite members of the English working class or lower middle class. They will unite in pursuit of a common interest, and in opposition to a common foe. But the unity will last only as long as the threat, and extend only as far as is necessary to deal with the threat. Often activists have despaired as the carefully constructed unity in a common cause has evaporated when the immediate target has been achieved but before the great leap forward which will change the world. Activists and idealists have pursued something akin to solidarity, while my English compatriots seek peace and privacy.

So I suggest solidarity of the oppressed must be replaced in an English liberation theology by some concept of common interest of the excluded. This is much less attractive, much less inspiring, much narrower in scope: but it does resonate with those who need liberation.

5. Exclusion, fairness and common interest - Liberation Theology?

It is clear that these three concepts are linked together, indeed are mutually supportive, as are oppression , justice and solidarity. Thus an important factor in the feeling of exclusion is the idea that it is unfair for people to have the power to exclude others from benefits simply by virtue of accident of birth. Part of the notion of public accountability and private conduct would not work without a clear understanding of fairness and a trust that fairness will operate, and the idea of common interest would not attract any support were it not believed that the fruits of the struggle would be fairly distributed. Many of the struggles which have united the working class and lower middle class people have been struggles against exclusivity or unfairness.

The links between these three concepts are significant for my purpose, for they mean that you cannot embrace or replace any one of the trio without taking account of the others. So if I am correct in claiming that these ideas are more useful for an English liberation theology than oppression, justice and solidarity, we must take them as a package and recognise their common deep roots.

It would be easier if they were not so entwined. Superficially, there are resemblances, between justice and aspects of fairness, and between solidarity and common interest. It would be convenient to select those aspects which look alike and work with them, adjusting the theology of liberation where appropriate. Instead, if my claims hold water, we must undertake a much larger and more radical revision of liberation theology for an English (and hence British) context.

One way of starting to explore a theology of liberation which takes account of the concepts I have been outlining is to turn to the Bible. Are there are any echoes of these notions there?

It is fairly easy to claim that the Gospels are non-exclusive. Even Jesus was rebuked, by a woman, for refusing to minister to non-Jews. The rest of the New Testament contains much that seem to be against exclusivity. The Old Testament is a different matter: there we find everything from total exclusiveness, including the destruction of those who do not belong to the favoured race, to a vision of total inclusiveness. However, I cannot find much support for any serious attempt to open the fences of existing magic circles. I do find a great deal, especially in the Old Testament, which supports the idea of including people in existing circles of privilege - especially me, Lord!

What I have described as fairness is akin, it seems to me, to the biblical concept of justice. It is about equality, and it is not about treating everybody alike. Rather, justice in the Bible, like fairness, is about treating everyone according to their character and proper deserts. Like fairness, biblical justice is a very loose concept, and what is regarded, apparently by God, as just on one occasion is not seen as just on another. Both Testaments contain instants of rank injustice, which nevertheless seem quite fair in context! One might even be really tendentious, and claim that the concept of fairness is a better expression of the triumph of grace over law than any concept of justice: but that would be to swallow completely the peculiarly English view that justice and law are cosy partners.

When we reach the ideas of privacy, public accountability and common interest, we meet greater biblical difficulties. The Gospel insists that all will be revealed, and the things which people would prefer to hide away will be brought into the open. There is no idea that you can do in private what you would not do in public. Public accountability there is certainly, but it is a public accountability for all our life. And with that openness to scrutiny goes an openness to others which demands that you are available to them, and so are your possessions. The Gospels seem to demand a total commitment, to Jesus and to the followers of Jesus, which sits uneasily with the idea of coming together for brief bouts of pursuit of a common interest.

However, there is no suggestion that total openness should be forced on one, at least in this life. The rich young ruler is allowed to walk sadly away, someone is allowed to stay rich enough to provide Jesus with a tomb, and even in the primitive communism of the early Acts of the Apostles, it is up to individuals how much they give and how much they keep. As for commitment, one wonders how Jesus viewed Nicodemus.

So maybe there are biblical elements on which we can draw to create a theology which takes account of English reserve. But would the resulting theology be a theology of liberation? I am not sure. I am sure that these, my people, need liberation, and I am sure that theology ought to be able to help them to find their liberation - somehow.

ANDREW BRADSTOCK

LIBERATION THEOLOGY AFTER THE FAILURE OF REVOLUTION

Andrew Bradstock is Lecturer in Theology at the LSU
College of Higher Education, an accredited college of
Southampton University. A frequent visitor to South
America, his last visit was in December 1994

1. After Nicaragua 1990

The Sandinistas' loss of power at the elections in February 1990, suspending - or , as is would now seem, terminating - the revolution in Nicaragua, was viewed with sadness, frustration and anger by many who had seen in that process signs of a new and innovative model of development for countries of the so-called Third World. The circumstances which led to the abandonment of the revolution have been analysed often enough, and will not be picked over again here; rather we shall explore the possible consequences of this even for the future of liberation theology (both here and in Latin America), given that the revolution was enthusiastically endorsed by liberation theologians and articulated many of the central concerns of that theology. Does the collapse of the revolution challenge liberation theology to rethink its long-held commitment to structural transformation? Does it contain warnings for Christians committed to seeing kingdom values rooted historically in their society? What implications does it have for the outworking of an option for the poor? In considering these questions we need also to take into account developments in the world at large, not least the ending of the Cold War and consequent discrediting of Marxism and socialism and growth in influence of economic liberalism. Whither liberation theology under this new world order?

We need spend only the briefest moment sketching in the background to the matters we shall be considering; events in Nicaragua from the late 1970s to the early 1990s were given a reasonably high profile - even in our own chronically parochial media - at the time, and have been well documented and analysed since. Suffice to say that in July 1979, in what was the first revolutionary transfer of power in the region since Castro landed on Cuba twenty years before, the Sandinista Front led a popular uprising in Nicaragua, ending the Somoza dictatorship and setting in motion a process of social transformation which, even within its first year, had begun to improve the accessibility of health care, education, the land and other vital service and resources. Playing a significant role in this process, at all levels, were churchpeople of all denominations, who perceived in the revolutionary leadership a commitment to make effective, on a social scale, the gospel

89

imperative to feed the hungry, care for the sick and clothe the naked. Within a short time, however, the revolution became derailed, due in large part to the inability of the new Reagan administration in the USA to comprehend it except within the context of Soviet expansionism. Sensing a threat to the 'peace' and 'stability' of its backyard, Reagan pledged to have the Sandinistas out of office before the end of his own presidency, employing economic sanctions, the mining of Nicaragua ports, and the organisation and financing of an armed counter-revolutionary force, the *contra*, to fulfil his aim. In the end he missed his deadline by only a matter of weeks as the Nicaraguan people, bloodied and bowed by a war which had cost them their hopes, their dreams and the lives of many of their families and friends, voted in February 1990 to call off the revolution. An analysis of that election cannot ignore the contribution the Sandinistas made to their own unpopularity in the form of, for example, incompetence and inefficiency in economic matters and insensitivity towards the Miskito Indians on the Atlantic Coast; yet few observers would seriously dispute that uppermost in the minds of most Nicaraguans as they went to the polls was the war, its grim consequences, and what could be done to end it.

The election brought to power an anti-Sandinista coalition of fourteen widely disparate parties - with the singularly inappropriate acronym UNO - under the presidency of Dona Violetta Chamorro, widow of a newspaper editor who had been assassinated shortly before the triumph in 1978. The Sandinista Front, however, remained the largest single part, a fact which encouraged many observers to hope that, at the next elections in 1996, they would return to office and kick-start the revolution back into life. Subsequent developments, however, have removed such hopes from all but the most optimistic breast; a process of reassessment by former Sandinista sympathisers has led many to question the suitability of revolution as a vehicle for political change; the Sandinista leadership has lost much of its moral standing, not lease by its involvement in a crude and cynical land-grab - known as *la pinata* - between losing the election and handing over power; the Front has recently endured a major and seemingly irreparable split over fundamental issues of ideology. Recent opinion polls suggest that not only have the Sandinistas no realistic chance of being re-elected next year, the one faction which *does* would lead the country in an even more right-ward direction than the present administration.

So what lessons, warnings, and inspiration can we draw from all of this? I want to highlight what seem to be three important strands which emerge from the Nicaraguan experience and explore what they have to say to us, though one or two observations should be made first.

To begin, and this has been said often enough , we must be wary of trying to lift the experience of people in one location in order to apply it simplistically to our own. Gutierrez himself has argued that every theology 'to the extent that it springs from an experience that is both deeply human and deeply Christian .. is a question and challenge for believers living in other human situations.'(1) Liberation theology, if it is anything, is a contextual theology, a response to and reflection upon praxis undertaken in given historical circumstances; and the priority given to praxis (in respect of chronology, not status) means that the most applicable responses to any situation will emerge from within that situation itself, and not be available beforehand in the form of theories or theologies fashioned elsewhere.

Second, we must beware of over-reacting to the events we are considering. Nicaraguans have been through an almost unimaginable series of traumatic experiences in the last two decades, culminating in the sudden, and for many unexpected disintegration of the Sandinista experiment, and it is no surprise that many who were once caught up in the process are rethinking profoundly their whole commitment to liberation theology and even the Christian faith itself. The reasons underlying their responses and reactions are too complex to explore here, but suffice to say that there may be lessons which we, enjoying a privileged detachment from their experience, may learn from it in terms of clinging, in the face of despair, to that hope in a God greater than our situation and the eventual triumph of life over death.

Third, we must recognise how open and fluid the present is. In the last six years we have witnessed in Eastern Europe, the former Soviet Union and southern Africa, as well as Latin America, events which have turned those parts of the world almost literally upside down, and there is little to suggest things are more settled now as we approach the third millenium. Any lessons we may draw today we must therefore hold in an attitude of openness to the new ones which will emerge tomorrow, and in that sense (among others!) this paper must be seen as very much a 'working' document. Finally, exploring these questions should be no mere academic exercise, but one relevant to our own praxis to further the reign of God where we are.

2. Reading the signs of the times

The first point to make - and, though hardly new, it is as relevant now as ever - concerns the importance of discerning the signs of the times and the extent to which Christian praxis must adapt in response to them. The point follows from the third of the preliminary ones made above, and emerges from a conviction, expressed by many churchpeople in Nicaragua and elsewhere in Latin America today, that the profound transformation which the world has recently undergone now suggests a radically different agenda for those committed to an option for the poor and the central tenets of liberation theology. We need do no more than summarise the main elements of this transformation; the collapse of 'really existing socialism' in the old Soviet Union and Eastern Europe; the discrediting, in the popular perception at least, of Marxism as a workable ideology; the growth, partly in consequence of the disappearance of a countervailing superpower, of United States hegemony on the global stage; the increasingly influential role in the 'third' as well as the 'first' world of the International Monetary Fund and the World bank; and the growth in popularity of the economic theory of neo-liberalism, not least in the form of the 'structural adjustment policies' which the IMF promotes in developing countries as the solution to all their ills. From any perspective these developments have given the world a different face, and from the south a somewhat threatening one. They also pose new challenges to those committed to an option for the poor.

Some churchpeople in Nicaragua have seen the transformations which occurred in Eastern Europe and their own country as part of a single historical process which has redefined what is realistically possible. To put things very bluntly, before 1989 Marxist-inspired revolutions and centrally-planned economies were on the agenda; now they are not. In the 1970s churchpeople viewed support for the Sandinista project to be not only consistent with a Christian commitment to see the values of the kingdom reflected in society, but the project itself as one likely to succeed in actually creating a new social order predicated on those values. For some, in fact, it was the *only* route to the establishment of Christian values in a society so seriously fractured and dehumanised by years of corrupt and brutal government. At Medellin in 1968 the Latin American bishops had spoken of the 'unjust structures' in many of the countries on their continent and of the need for the transformation (2) (a perspective already shared and subsequently developed by liberation theologians), and to many Nicaraguan Christians the revolutionary movement in their country appeared committed precisely to bringing about such a structural transformation. In addition, the absence of any experience of genuine democratic participation under Somoza, the failure of successive 'development' programmes emanating from the United States, and the example of a surviving revolutionary model in their own region, namely Cuba, only underlined the imperative of commitment to a revolutionary transformation.(3)

Now, it is argued, revolution is off the agenda. Notwithstanding a continued measure of support for the Sandinistas and the resurgence of Communist ideas in some Eastern European countries, the events of 1989 and 1990 have brought to an end an era in which the fashioning of new social orders from the embers of revolutionary struggle could be seriously regarded. 'Macro' responses to injustice and poverty no longer 'work', or, perhaps more precisely, are allowed to work.

A consequence of those events has been the discrediting of socialism and Marxism as bases for a sustainable and democratic political order, and acquisition of greater credibility by capitalism and 'democracy' - as defined in Western liberal terms - something hailed in (almost) apocalyptic terms by some as the logical denouement of history. Neo-liberalism, the ultimate laisser-faire economic system, is now the order of the day, proposing in total contrast to the Marxism of Eastern Europe, the free and unfettered operation of the market, and minimal interference from the state, as the panacea for all economic ills. In the new world order power resides, not primarily with the transnationals, but with the IMF and World Bank, with technocrats in the major cities of the world rather than the owners of capital themselves.(4) The Chamorro government in Nicaragua espouses neo-liberal policies, and the country, having successfully carried through two 'free and fair' elections in the last ten years, might now be said to have embraced Western, multi-party democracy. But what sort of challenges do these developments pose to Christians there and indeed all who embrace liberation theology and an option for the poor?

First, we need to challenge the notion that there is a continuity between events in Eastern Europe in 1989 and Nicaragua in 1990. The systems in both regions might have been labelled 'Marxist', but such was the contrast between the monolithic and over-bureaucratised societies presided over by the Communist parties in the Warsaw bloc, and the pluralist and participatory process in Nicaragua, the use of the term has little real meaning. It was also unclear whether, in Nicaragua, people felt antipathy toward the system itself, as in Eastern Europe, or voted for respite from the external pressures on it. Francis McDonagh would therefore seem to be right when he says that 'the fall of institutional Marxism in Eastern Europe... [has] only marginal relevance to the Latin American church...'(5). The collapse of Communism in Eastern Europe did not necessarily say anything about the validity of liberation theologians' own agenda for a new order, since all that was lost was one particular manifestation of socialism, one which most liberation theologians would clearly distinguish from their own vision of a just society.(6) Like Chesterton's 'Christian ideal' the socialism of liberation

93

theology has not been tried and found wanting, but found difficult and left untried.

3. Liberation Theology without Marxism

But even if Marxism and Socialism are now perceived to be discredited, were they so pivotal to the liberation project that their demise must drag that project down with them? The testimony of liberation theologians themselves would suggest not. Although Socialism is generally seen by liberation theologians in a positive light - McGovern, for example, claims that he has yet to find any who do not favour it in some form (7) - few would now define it as essential to liberation theology. Jose Libanio, for example, prefers to talk of 'alternatives to capitalism' rather than socialism. (8) and Gutierrez, who included positive if cautious references to socialism in some of his early work, has more recently stated that ' one can support liberation theology or do liberation theology without espousing socialism.'(9)

Liberation theology's commitment to Marxism has also waned. Since Marx's critique related to a stage of capitalism further advanced than that reached in Latin America, its applicability to that region was always questionable. Many liberation theologians, latching onto a distinction found particularly in Althusser between Marxism as 'ideology' and 'science', did claim to find in Marx's critique of capitalism and Lenin's theory of imperialism valuable tools for analysing a Latin American society still dependent on an economic system directed from the First World. Few, however, embraced Marxism - notwithstanding the Vatican's insistence that one could not take one part of Marxism without the whole ideology.(10) And none claimed it to be *integral* to liberation theology. Indeed , some have recently argued that Marxist language can be jettisoned without undermining the central tenets of liberation theology, that Marxism is just *one* method of analysing social change, and that sources of oppression other than those based on class, for example sexual and racial, need to addressed. Liberation theologians remain firmly and radically anti-capitalist and anti-imperialist, but not necessarily pro-Marxist or even dependent on Marxism. As Dussel argues, 'If its purpose of liberating the poor and oppressed of the Latin American continent requires a revitalised form of Marxism, it will be able to produce this, if not, it will not need it.'(11)

This notwithstanding, liberation theology still has to take cognizance of the perceived loss of credibility which Marxian and other forms of socialism have suffered since 1989, together with the apparently inexorable forward march of neo-liberal economics and western-style democracy. Even if

94

liberation theology is not dependent on Marxism or socialism, it cannot ignore the fact that during the 1980s a significant shift to the right occurred on an almost global scale, challenging popular assumptions about the role and scope of the market, the feasibility and desirability of 'social' transformation, and even whether an entity called society could be held to exist. The influence of the market now extends further than could ever have been imagined fifteen or twenty years ago, to the extent that the 'victory' of capitalism over socialism has been hailed as bringing us effectively to (in Francis Fukayama's arresting phrase) 'The End of History and the Last Man'. For Fukayama 'the unabashed victory of economic and political liberalism' over all its competitors implies 'not just the end of the cold war, or the passing of a particular period in history, but the end of history as such; that is, the end-point of mankind's ideological evolution and the universalisation of Western liberal democracy.'(12) In an almost neo-Hegelian tone Fukayama identifies an underlying evolutionary direction to history, the end state of which, liberal democratic and capitalist society, has now been reached.(13) As David McLellan comments, 'Fukayama did not claim that the end of history yielded a perfect society - only that there was no prospect of a better alternative to liberal capitalism ... [he] was not claiming that there will be no more events, but only that the final conceptual and political framework in which these events would take place had already been achieved...'(14) This theses gains added plausibility not only because the 'unabashed victory of economic and political liberalism' has removed a (potential) counterweight on the world stage to the expansionist aspiration of the capitalist nations, but because the collapse of the Socialist states of Eastern Europe has resulted in the loss of a model of an alternative to the status quo.

It is hard to argue, in other words, that the end of the Cold War has not left us with an overall impression of the defeat of alternative s to capitalism, which is of course exactly how that event is viewed from the right. Jorge Castaneda spells this out clearly in his survey of the current state of the Latin American left, *Utopia Unarmed*: 'the collapse of socialism meant the loss of a paradigm', he writes' the self-destruction of the basic model signified the disappearance of the left's framework for conceiving of an alternative to Latin America's current state of affairs'. 'The idea of revolution ... has lost its meaning ... [it] has withered and virtually died because its outcome has become either unwanted or unimaginable. Equally important, after the Nicaragua elections of 1990, revolution has become reversible'. Further, the collapse of socialism 'accelerated ... and enhanced the attractiveness' of the free-market model of economic development over against the state-controlled alternative one.(15)

4. Responding to Neo-Liberalism

How is liberation theology to respond to neo-liberalism's new agenda, which seeks to remove even from the realm of political discourse, the possibility of structural transformation in the interest of the poor (such as that attempted in Nicaragua)? The dilemma is a real one for all movements of the left at this particular point in history, including those within our country. Should they respond to the contemporary ideological shift by going some way towards embracing the 'market-culture'; hold firmly to traditional socialist values and risk becoming increasingly irrelevant; or seek a difficult twilight position in between.

For most liberation theologians, the first option of accommodation with neo-liberalism and all its works has to be rejected, not because liberation theology is frozen into a relationship with one particular (and now defunct) political ideology,(16) but because any other stance would undermining liberation theology's raison d'etre as a theology of the poor. Few Latin American theologians would perhaps go as far as Franz Hinkelammert in speaking of capitalism committing 'mass murder among the working classes' and sucking the blood of living labour, but many recognise that poverty has become even more severe and widespread in their region during the recent years of capitalism's greater freedom. Rodolfo Cardenal writes, with no little irony, that 'the downfall of historic socialisms ...[has] ... not automatically implied the liberation of the exploited and oppressed majorities',(17) and Xabier Gorostiaga has shown in some detail how the change of axis the world experienced in November 1989 was to the detriment of the poor in the developing world.(18) For theologians and observers alike the roots of the worsening situation for millions in the developing world are traceable directly to the new economic policies of the right. Indeed, increased un- or under-employment, falling incomes and reduced life chances are perceived to be the inevitable consequences of the outworking of these policies. As Professor James Dunkerley of the Institute of Latin American Studies in London points out in a recent paper, 18 months after the election of Violetta Chamorro, whose UNO coalition government is committed to neo-liberalism and structural adjustment, the state of the poor in Nicaragua ' was still the worst in the isthmus, with some 50 per cent of the labour force un- or under-employed and over 69 per cent unable to meet basic food needs.'(19) Speaking in London in October 1994 the Managua-based economist Isolda Espinosa noted some further consequences of the structural adjustment policies to which Nicaragua had been subjected since 1990. 'We have seen the average wage, which in 1990 covered 90% of the basic basket of goods, drop in 1992 to 72%,' she said, going on to quote United Nations statistics which showed that 'by the end of 1991, 70% of the Nicaraguan population were living in poverty, of which 40% were living in conditions of extreme poverty.'(20)

Endless statistics could be quoted to give added weight to this argument, though none will adequately convey the social, physical, psychological and environmental consequences of this trend; the phenomenal growth in crime (currently rising at six times the birth rate),(21) sickness and premature death (including the return of cholera after more than a hundred years),(22) homelessness (which often leads to deforestation as the landless go in search of new pastures),(23) prostitution, drug-trafficking, falling education standards' - in short, near total social disintegration. It will be argued, of course, that neo-liberalism achieves truly remarkable results in terms of combating inflation, and few governments can match the Chamorro coalition's achievement of reducing inflation in Nicaragua from 13,500% to single figures within a couple of years of coming to office. Such results cannot be achieved without some short-term hardship , it will be conceded, but in the long-term everyone benefits more than they would under the sort of hyper-inflation which the Sandinistas presided over (which reached its peak at around 33,500%).

Yet liberation theology's fundamental problem with neo-liberalism is its *orientation*. Whose concerns, it asks, are prioritised by neo-liberal governments? Whose interests are their policies really designed to serve? Do they share with liberation theologians a concern to make life - the life of the poor - the criterion, in Pablo Richard's words ' for discerning what is *rational* and what is *irrational*'?(24) Capitalism by its very nature cannot put people before profitability: as Duncan Green argues in his forthcoming study of the rise of market economics in Latin America, 'the overriding freedom in the neo-liberal canon is that of the "free" market, and where freeing the market is incompatible with freeing the people, the market usually takes precedence.'(25) What most liberation theologians have always maintained, that there is an irresolvable conflict between the logic of capitalism and an option for the poor, and that capitalism is therefore fundamentally beyond reform, appears even more obviously true of what is perhaps its ultimate expression, neo-liberalism. Few would challenge Leonardo Boff's assertion that 'Capitalism can be more or less immoral; it can never be more or less moral', or that 'it is just as impossible to create a moral market system as it is to build a Christian brothel'!(26) Thus as Dussel maintains, 'faced with the massive scale of the progressive "impoverishment" of Latin America under the recessive peripheral capitalist system imposed by the World Bank and the IMF, theology must remain true to its ability to express the 'cry of the oppressed'.(27) It will not do this, however, if it allows itself to be seduced by those who are part of the problem masquerading as custodians of the solution.

The subtlety of neo-liberalism's challenge to liberation theology extends even so far as presenting itself in the guise of an alternative 'option for the poor. In a paper read to a gathering of theologians in San Jose, Costa Rica, in January 1995, Franz Hinkelammert reported a claim by the Director General of the IMF, Michel Camdessus, in 1992, that the mandate of his organisation was to fulfil the promise of Isaiah which Jesus adopted at the start of his ministry (Like 4. 18-19): "the Spirit of the Lord is upon me, because he has anointed me to bring good news to the poor ..." In line with the received wisdom in neo-liberal circles, Camdessus argued that the market offered, not just the most efficient economic means for increasing individual and corporate wealth, but the only means: to want any other policy than that pursued by the IMF was to want the increase of poverty. As Hinkelammert comments, this amounts to nothing less than a claim that 'who is for the poor must be for the Fund. There are no alternatives ...' The option for the poor is transformed into an option for the IMF. 'The "new man" has returned, but he is now an official of the IMF'!(28)

5. A Restated Liberation Theology

For some liberation theologians neo-liberal claims to be on the side of the poor border on the blasphemous. Hinkelammert himself refers to the 'anti-theology of the IMF', and Rodolfo Cardenal, vice-rector of the University of Central America in San Salvador, views talk that we have reached the best of all possible worlds as symptomatic of the predominance of the 'anti-reign' with 'its fundamental values of resignation, adaptation to reality and inevitability'.(29) Jorge Pixley is another who is uncompromising in his critique of capitalism, denouncing the market as satanic insofar as its success depends on causing unemployment, sickness and ultimately death. 'A market which condemns the majority to live in subhuman misery cannot be a government put there by God' he said in a sermon delivered in December 1994 at the Baptist seminary in Managua where he lectures. Pixley also compared present-day capitalism, with its aspiration to rule the world, with the 'pax romana' of the first century, and called on Christians today to resist the former as their forebears in the faith did the latter in their own time. Such a stand - which Pixley compared to withstanding the mark of the beast in the Book of Revelation - will make life difficult if not impossible, but in the light of the first commandment resistance can be the only response to a market which thinks it is god. Liberation theologians have for a long time been unmasking pretensions of divinity on the part of all sorts of ideology, and as

Rosemary Radford Ruether has recently written, ' the real struggle of faith today is not the conflict between theism and atheism, but between the true God and the idols. The idols clothe war and injustice, violence and oppression, in religious mantles and claim that these come forth from the hand of God.'(30)

For Pixley, liberation theology needs not only to maintain a stance of dogged resistance to neo-liberalism, it can also continue to talk about 'socialist projects'. But for how long will political and economic discourse still be conducted in terms of this sort, either in Latin America or elsewhere? As the poor become more and more attracted or seduced by the prospects offered by the ideology of the market, particularly when dressed in religious clothes as a 'prosperity gospel', can liberation theology afford to remain shouting from the sidelines, fighting new battles with old ideas and slogans? Given that sweeping 'instant' solutions are now no longer practicable or even attractive, should it not look for new socio-economic models which can still make effective an option for the poor?

Pixley himself recognises that the old Exodus paradigm, which was perhaps the most powerful in liberation theology (and about which he once wrote a major treatise)(31) must now be viewed in a different light, and some in Nicaragua find it more helpful today to reflect on the Babylonian captivity. In the Exodus narrative the people of God were bowed down by oppression, but were led, eventually, to liberation in a new land. In Babylon, however, where they experienced the loss of their political, social and cultural autonomy, their dreams of liberation were not focused on new territory but the rebuilding of their community. And for lay Catholic theologian Jose Arguello this is the task for the church today, to return to working alongside the poor at grass-roots level and looking for small successes rather than grand global ones (though together small successes could make an impact).(32) A particularly powerful theme of the Babylonian captivity narrative, argues Arguello, was the role of the small prophetic remnant, who called on their leaders to recover their moral authority and return to the Lord by showing a concern for the poor. Interestingly the rise of neo-liberalism, with its emphasis on a minimal role for the state, helps to create the space and opportunity for the church to engage precisely in this work of building community: in some areas of Nicaragua, particularly the countryside, the church is the only network that can organise people. Finding many in the church who have worked alongside the poor full of frustration, resentment, despair and resignation in the wake of recent events, Arguello argues that this work of empowering the poor and rebuilding community is one which is both possible and necessary for the church.

The Protestant theologian Roberto Zub, Dean of the Faculty of Theology at the Inter-Church Centre for Theological and Social Studies (CIEETS) in Managua, has also spoken of the need for the church to move away from seeking solutions at the level of the general and think, for the present anyway, on a much smaller scale. 'I don't believe in any global solution at this time', he has said: ' first you have to sort out the particular, and hopefully in time that will affect the general.'(33) Zub is one who sees 'revolution' in a very different light from before: it was totally mistaken, he argues, to expect the revolution to solve every problem: the concern now must be to develop society sector by sector, though if all these sectors are developed to a certain standard then that is revolution and that will work.

The phenomenal growth of evangelicalism in Nicaragua (and indeed the whole continent of Latin America)(34) increases the imperative for churchpeople with a liberation perspective to continue to work closely with the poor. Not all evangelical churches are politically reactionary or interested only in saving souls for the next life: according to Gustavo Parajon, director of the Protestant development agency CEPAD, some 75% of the country's nearly 100 evangelical groupings work with his organisation , which opted for the revolution in the 1980s and continues to support development projects and community organisation in poorer areas.(35) But some do preach a highly individualistic theology and life-style, self-consciously undermining liberation theology's emphasis on a God who saves whole peoples, and attract disaffected Catholics by making available what their own church (or at least its hierarchy) no longer appears to value, including a sense of community.

The call for a 'politics of community' can also be heard from within our own first world context, with its profoundly different opportunities and possibilities. Jim Wallis, for example, observes that we are in a time of transition, 'stranded between paradigms', and need to look, not for 'new macroeconomic systems' to replace the failed 'ideological dinosaurs' of the past, but for ways to ensure that new politics and projects 'empower the powerless, protect the earth, and foster true democracy'.(36) Although the old ideological frameworks of left and right are inadequate for today, Wallis argues, their loss creates space for an 'independent spiritual voice for social justice and reconciliation': a prophetic vision which is 'political without being ideological' and which makes 'genuine citizen participation' rather than 'passive public polling' the 'defining practice of our political system.'(37) A weakness of Wallis' position is of course that ideological frameworks of the right will not disappear just because we wish them to; the left will still need tools to fashion critiques of the causes of poverty and marginalisation in society. But his vision is one worth exploring by those concerned to make real and relevant an option for the poor in our present context.

6. 'Be Ye Separate...'

A second lesson which emerges from the experience of the failure of the Nicaraguan revolution - though some may question how much relevance it has for us in Britain as the moment! - is the imperative for the church and individual Christians not to become *absorbed* into secular movements and parties, however close the values of those movements appear to be to their own.

This is not to suggest that the church should not align with movements outside in order to realise its goals: even as Luther once observed, ' Christians are not so many that they can get together in mobs!(38) Nor is it specifically to condemn Christians in Nicaragua who joined or worked closely with the Sandinista Front. Given the Front's clearly-stated commitment to build a new social order embodying values consistent with those of the gospel and the dignity of the human person, Christian participation in the revolutionary project can be easily defended.

Rather, it is to warn against the danger of what Gutierrez has called 'baptising' any political movement with the name 'Christian',(39) of reducing Christianity without remainder to any one secular project and identifying with it so closely that all hope for the realisation of gospel values is invested in it, leaving no space on which to stand to judge it. Many in Nicaragua who travelled with the Sandinistas have since reflected profoundly on that experience and concluded that, not only does such collaboration no longer seem appropriate in the light of the movement's loss of the moral highground it once held, but precisely because all political movements have the potential to lose their original ideals it is always mistaken for the church to identify too closely with them. The problem is not that the party concerned had Marxist or atheistic strands in its ideology, but that Christians themselves invested too much faith and trust in one particular movement, some even to the extent of believing it could ba a vehicle to actualise the kingdom of God - which had serious consequences for their faith once that movement ran aground.

7. The hope of the Kingdom

It is vital, then, to keep a vision of the Kingdom always before us.

Whilst the defeat of the revolution in Nicaragua has left some bereft of hope that the Kingdom of God can be realised even partially in history, hope in the Kingdom is one thing we should not lose hold of, grounded as it in the promise of the Lord. 'Those who think that the liberating utopia of the Kingdom is impossible and would abandon it, should be reminded that Christians believe that it was inaugurated in the resurrection of Jesus', Rodolfo Cardenal has said.(40) A key word here is utopia, which Cardenal defines as 'not that which does not happen, but that which has a place in this world but is denied, repressed, invaded and dominated by another foreign force'.(41) Indeed, the main characteristic of utopia, as Gutierrez has argued, is 'its relationship to present historical reality': it is both a denunciation of the status quo and an annunciation of what is to come.(42)

The Kingdom of God, then, should stir the utopian imagination to affirm both the non-necessity of the imperfect present and the hope of a new and better order, and liberation theology needs to stress that all is *not* sewn up, that we have *not* reached the best possible world, a task made all the more urgent and necessary by the suffering of the poor under the present order. Liberation theology must be more utopian than ever, as Berryman says, 'within the context of the new international order, which radically destroys all utopias.'(43) But the Kingdom can only retain its utopian dimension so long as its permanently eschatological character - in the sense that it is both 'here' and 'not yet' - is not lost sight of, and the temptation to imagine it can be fully realised here and now through one particular historical struggle is avoided.

Although events in Nicaragua and elsewhere have brought a loss of faith in politicians and political solutions, and a loss of hope in alternatives and utopias, liberation theology must continue to be pledged 'to regain the utopia of the Gospel in the face of those who believe there is nothing more to hope for.'(44) It has a message of hope to fill the void of hopelessness opened up by the loss of movements which once promised so much, because its vision is greater than any one movement and its hope is grounded in a God greater than all our projects, conceptualisations, and models for change. A statement signed by 148 priests in Nicaragua after the 1990 elections captures well this sense of hope: 'This is the hour for Christians in Latin America. We Christians know that Jesus was faithful to the God of the poor, although all horizons closed in and the Empire crucified him. God and the gospel have not changed. Let us remain faithful. The Kingdom of God is at hand. Let us be converted and believe in the good news (Mark 1:15)'.(45)

In her contribution to the *Festschrift* prepared for Gustavo Gutierrez's sixtieth birthday, Maria Clara Bingemer compares the uttering of women's theological message 'amid the formerly monolithic and impregnable structure of male theology' to the pouring of ointment at the feet of Jesus by the woman at Bethany.(46) Is this not also a picture of how liberation theology should speak today against the 'monolithic and impregnable structure' of discourse about the end of history and impossibility of alternatives? Must our theology not continue to have, as she puts it, 'the courage to pour out the perfume at someone else's party', to keep a plurality of scents in the environment even though they will sometimes be incompatible and often in conflict?

Footnotes

1. Gustavo Gutierrez, A Theology of Liberation, ET London: SCM, 2nd ed. 1988, p.xxxvi
2. The Church in the Present-Day Transformation of Latin America in the Light of the Council: Conclusions, Washington DC: 3rd ed. 1,2,3.
3. cf. Francis McDonagh, Accents in Theology, New Blackfriars (72:1991), p.434
4. Duncan Green gives an insight into Latin America's new breed of technocrat in Silent Revolution: The Rise of Market Economics in Latin America, London: LAB/Cassell, 1995
5. McDonagh, loc. cit., p.435
6. Arthur McGovern, Liberation Theology is alive and well, The Tablet, 15 September 1990, p.1156; idem, Liberation Theology and its Critics, NY: Orbis, 1989, p.xix
7. McGovern, Liberation Theology and its Critics, p.148
8. Cited in Paul E Sigmund, Liberation Theology at the Crossroads, Oxford: OUP, 1990, p.178
9. See, for example, A Theology of Liberation, ET London: SCM, 1974, pp.90, 111, 274; Liberation Praxis and Christian Faith, in R Gibellini (ed), Frontiers of Theology in Latin America, ET London: SCM, 1980, p.9; The Power of the Poor in History, ET London: SCM,1983, p.45; McGovern, Liberation Theology and its Critics, p 148.
10. The Congregation for the Doctrine of the Faith, Instruction on Certain Aspects of the "Theology of Liberation", 6 August 1984, VII.6.

11. Enrique Dussel, Recent Latin American Theology, in idem., The Church in Latin America: 1492-1992, Tunbridge Wells: Burns & Oates, and NY: Orbis, 1992, p.399.

12. Francis Fukayama, The End of History?, The National Interest, 16:1992, p.3; cited in David McLellan, Ideology, Buckingham: Open University Press, 2nd ed., 1994, p.75

13. On the question of the extent to which Latin America has embraced Western-style democracy Dunkerley has claimed (after Whitehead) that whereas in 1989 there were just two dictatorships in the region, 15 years earlier there had been just three constitutional governments; James Dunkerley, The Pacification of Central America, Research Paper 34 (extract), University of London, Institute of Latin American Studies, 1995, p.5

14. McLellan, op. cit., p.75

15. Jorge G. Castaneda, Utopia Unarmed: The Latin American Left After the Cold War, NY: Vintage, 1993, pp244/5, 241

16. Gutierrez has written of liberation theology's need, in the light of changing circumstances, to 'refine [its] analytical tools and develop new ones', and has recognised the inadequacy of dependency theory for an understanding of the problem of poverty in Latin America today; (A Theology of Liberation, 2nd ed., p.xxiv; cf. p.xliv; McGovern, Liberation Theology and Its Critics, p.117)

17. Rodolfo Cardenal, The Timeliness and the Challenge of the Theology of Liberation, in Reclaiming Vision: Education, Liberation and Justice. Papers of the Inaugural Summer School, July 1994, Southampton: LSU, 1994, p.19

18. Xabier Gorostiaga, Ya Comenzo el siglo XXI: el norte contra el sur, envio, 116:1991, pp.34-49

19. Dunkerley, loc.cit., p.14. In a paper read at the Central America in New World Context conference in London on 10 January 1995 Nicaraguan economist Arturo Grigsby suggested that the general level of unemployment in his country may have now risen to 66%.

20. Isolda Espinosa, Impact of structural adjustment on women, in Challenging the "New World Order": Popular Struggles in Central America. Day School Report, London: 1994, p.2.

21. Dunkerley, loc.cit., p.21

22. ibid., pp17/18

23. Grigsby has estimated that 4,000 square kilometres of rain forest are destroyed in the country each year in this way, (Central America in New World Context conference, London, January 1995)

24. Pablo Richard, Liberation Theology: A Difficult but Possible Future, in Marc H Ellis & Otto Maduro, ed., Expanding The View: Gustavo Gutierrez and The Future of Liberation Theology, NY: Orbis, 1989
25. Green, op.cit., chapter 1.
26. Cited in McGovern, Liberation Theology and its Critics, p.139
27. Dussel, loc.cit., p399
28. Franz J Hinkelammert, La teologia de la liberacion en el contexto economico-social de America Latina: Economica y teologia o la irracionalidad de lo racionalisado, unpublished paper, San Jose, Costa Rica, 1994. I am grateful to one of my students, David Olivero, for preparing a translation of this paper.
29. Hinkelammert, loc.cit.; Cardenal, loc.cit., p.23
30. Rosemary Radford Ruether, Religion and Society: Sacred Canopy vs. Prophetic Critique, in Ellis & Maduro, op.cit., p.75
31. George V. Pixley, On Exodus: A Liberation Perspective, ET NY: Orbis, 1987
32. Interview with the author, December 1994.
33. Interview with the author, December 1994.
34. A recent estimate by the Peruvian academic Samuel Escobar that Catholics in Latin America are converting to Protestantism at the rate of 400 per hour is widely held to be reliable. In Nicaragua it has been estimated that currently 30% of the population belongs to a non-Catholic denomination.
35. Interview with the author, December 1994.
36. Jim Wallis, The Soul of Politics, London: Harper Collins, 1994, pp5, xix
37. Ibid., pp.45-49
38. Cited in Gordon Rupp, Patterns of Reformation, London: Epworth Press, 1969, p.299
39. Cited in McGovern, Liberation Theology and its Critics, pp.133, 224
40. Cardenal, loc.cit., p.24
41. Ibid
42. Gutierrez, A Theology of Liberation, 1st ed., pp.232/3
43. Phillip Berryman, Stubborn Hope: Religion, Politics, and Revolution in Central America, NY: Orbis, 1994, pp.231/2
44. Cardenal, loc.cit., p.27
45. Cited in Dussel, From the Second Vatican Council to the Present Day, in idem (ed) op.cit., p.174
46. Maria Clara Bingemer, Women in the Future of the Theology of Liberation, in Ellis & Maduro, op.cit., p.178

NOTICEBOARD

THE INSTITUTE FOR
BRITISH LIBERATION THEOLOGY

The Institute for British Liberation Theology is an annual event at the Urban Theology Unit in Sheffield. People engaged in liberation theology practice and ministry are invited to bring papers and make presentations. Future Institutes will take place on Monday-Thursday 15-18 July 1996 and 21-24 July 1997, and in mid July of subsequent years.

Enquiries to the Director, Rev Dr John Vincent, 178 Abbeyfield Road, Sheffield S4 7AY

THE BRITISH LIBERATION THEOLOGY
CONSULTATION AND CELEBRATION

The British Liberation Theology Consultation and Celebration is a bi-annual event held at Wistaton Hall, near Crewe. It is a sharing and supportive fellowship for people working in liberation theology style projects and ministries. The next Consultation and Celebration will take place on Friday-Sunday 17-19 October 1997, then in October 1999.

Enquiries to the joint Co-ordinator, Mr Mike Simpson, 16 Wellington Road, Nantwich CW5 7BH

SOUTHAMPTON
CENTRE FOR CONTEMPORARY THEOLOGY
SUMMER SCHOOL

A Bi-annual Summer School is held at LSU Southampton. The first was "Reclaiming Vision: Education, Liberation and Justice", held in July 1994. The second is "Liberating the Vision", with sessions from Friday 24th to Tuesday 28th May, 1996.

Enquiries to the Secretary, Sonia Kendall, Department of Theology, LSU College of Higher Education, The Avenue, Southampton SO17 1BG

THE INSTITUTE FOR
BRITISH BLACK THEOLOGY

The Institute for British Black Theology is an annual meeting of workers and writers of British Black and Asian Theologies. Contributions are invited, which may become part of a proposed Journal. The Institute takes place at UTU in Sheffield. Future dates are Monday-Thursday 8-11 July 1996 and 14-17 July 1997, and in July of subsequent years.

Enquiries to the Chair, Rev Inderjit Bhogal, 210 Abbeyfield Road, Sheffield S4 7AZ

DOCTORAL PROGRAMME IN
CONTEXTUAL, URBAN AND LIBERATION THEOLOGIES

An MPhil/PhD course in Contextual, Urban and Liberation Theologies, with Dr John Vincent as Supervisor, is accredited by the Biblical Studies Department of Sheffield University, using the Urban Theology Unit as base. Groups of candidates meet for 3-day periods quarterly in Sheffield over the first two years of the part-time course.

Enquiries to the Supervisor, Rev Dr John Vincent, 178 Abbeyfield Road, Sheffield S4 7AY

URBAN THEOLOGY UNIT
LIBERATION THEOLOGY COURSES

Each Spring, two open 2-day courses in Liberation Theology - Third World, and in Liberation Theology - First World, take place at UTU, co-ordinated by John Vincent, Inderjit Bhogal and others.

Enquiries to the Administrator, Mr Peter Colby, UTU, 210 Abbeyfield Road, Sheffield, S4 7AZ

JOURNAL OF
BRITISH BLACK THEOLOGY

A Journal of British Black Theology will be published to provide an outlet and a forum for the exchange of theological ideas and reflection. The Journal will be a contribution to the development of Black Theology in Britain and elsewhere.

Contributions and enquiries to Rev Inderjit Bhogal, 210 Abbeyfield Road, Sheffield S4 7AZ

NOTE

Noticeboard items are welcome from all interested groups for possible inclusion in future volumes. Please send to British Liberation Theology, c/o Urban Theology Unit, 210 Abbeyfield Road, Sheffield S4 7AZ

THE URBAN THEOLOGY UNIT

The Urban Theology Unit was formed in 1969 as a resource for ministers and lay people engaged in Christian discipleship or ministry in the urban context. It has been based since 1973 in 3 Edwardian semi-detached houses on a pleasant but undeniably inner city street. UTU has provided a prophetic voice focussed particularly on the experience of inner city and housing estate workers and residents .

Some students are resident in the UTU houses for the duration of their course, but many more come in on a part time basis for a wide variety of short or longer courses. Opportunities exist for private study during sabbaticals etc. UTU also forms part of the Sheffield Federation of Centres for Bible, Theology and Mission Studies which includes the Church Army Wilson Carlile College, Cliff College, the Biblical Studies Dept. of Sheffield University and the Hallam Diocesan Adult Education Centre.

Courses

Current Courses are as follows:

The Diploma in Theology and Mission is the basic core course of UTU. It is half-time, and can be done whether in 1 year (the UTU Study Year), or over 2-3 years. It consists of 32 Wed-Thur sessions, 9.30 to 3.30, developing participants' theological perspectives, personal self-assessment, and discernment of future mission.

The Diploma in Ministry is a basic training course for ministerial trainees of all denominations. The course is part-time, over 3-4 years, with 6 integrative Theme Modules, 2 each year, plus a Denominational Seminar over 3 years and a Ministry Project.

The Bachelor of Ministry and Theology is a degree course accredited by Sheffield University providing a full or part-time professional training in church ministry, over 2-4 years.

MA, MPhil and PhD degrees may be taken at UTU with Dr John Vincent as Supervisor. The Master of Arts in Applied Biblical Studies is full time in one year or part time over two years. The Master of Philosophy (MPhil) and Doctor of Philosophy (PhD) in Contextual, Urban and Liberation Theologies are either full time or part time 1-6 years.

The Master of Ministry offers ordained ministers and others the opportunity to do further study in Ministry, and to work with their local church on a practical project. The degree takes 3-4 years. Each group meets bi-monthly, Mondays at 11am to Tuesdays at 4pm, either at UTU or regionally. A Doctorate in Ministry, taking selected MMin work forward to a doctoral level, will, hopefully, commence in 1996 or 1997.

The Diploma in Community Ministry is a course designed to meet the needs of Community Workers, Church workers and Ministers who desire a disciplined course closely related to their own ministry situation and community. 3 years of 10-12 days of work together in two 4-day periods at UTU plus day Regional Meetings.

Short Courses. Participants may take individual Modules in the Diploma and Bachelor Courses both in Theology and Mission and also in Ministry and Theology.

Students are encouraged to be involved in practical ministry alongside study, as the context of ministry and its practical implications are seen as vital elements of theological reflection. Liberation Theology forms an important core resource and methodology for most courses at UTU.

Resources

There are wide ranges of resources available at UTU in the extensive libraries and resource rooms. The General Library carries a range of books on contemporary issues and theology, while the Alan Dale Library has a large collection of Biblical Studies books. In addition the Periodicals Room has a huge array of current periodicals and back copies and the Resource Room has leaflets, cuttings and articles on a very diverse range of subjects.

UTU is a member unit of the Sheffield Inner City Ecumenical Mission, a grouping of inner city and housing estate churches and of alternative-style congregations. UTU has always operated on an ecumenical basis, drawing students and staff from different denominations and cultures. As an integral part of a group of churches and at the centre of a community of interested and associated people, UTU has a real place in the social fabric of its location.

UTU is a membership organisation. People from all over the country and overseas take an active interest in its life and work. Members are kept up-to-date with the developments at UTU and also receive new publications as they are produced. Basic membership is currently £20 per annum, or £12 low income. UTU is a Registered Charity (No. 505334). Publication of work in relation to the charitable aims of UTU has been an important aspect of our activity. Several new volumes are published each year.

UTU has a small Core Staff of 8, mainly part-time, with 30 graduates and associates acting as tutors on different courses. Rev Dr John Vincent has been Director since the creation of UTU, and Rev Inderjit Bhogal Director of Studies since 1994. Core Staff Lecturers currently are Rev Dr Ian Duffield, Rev Ed Kessler, Mrs Elizabeth Mitchell, Rev Dr Robin Pagan and Ms Jan Royan, with Mr Peter Colby as Administrator.

Write for details of membership and Courses to:

Urban Theology Unit, 210 Abbeyfield Road, Sheffield S4 7AZ. Telephone and Fax: 0114 243 5342.

UTU PUBLICATIONS

NEW CITY JOURNAL

18.	UTU in the 80s	£2.00
19.	A Petition of Distress from the Cities	£1.00

NEW CITY SPECIALS

1.	John Vincent	Strategies for Mission	.20p
2.	Consultation	Alternative Theological Education	£1.00
3.	John Vincent	Alternative Journeys	.60p
4.	Ed Kessler	Radical Jesus in Parables	.50p
5.	Marian Lowndes	A Mission in the City	£1.00
6.	John Vincent	Hymns of the City	£1.00
7.	John Vincent	Five Pillars of Christianity	.60p
8.	Margaret Walsh	Here's Hoping	£2.00
9.	John Vincent	Liberation Theology from the Inner City	£1.00
10.	Laurie Green	God in the Inner City	£2.00
11.	James Ashdown	Gentrification	£2.00

PEOPLE'S BIBLE STUDIES

1.	Ed Kessler	Secrets of the Parables 1. The Good Samaritan	£2.00
2.	John Vincent	Good News in Britain Five Gospel Stories seen Today	£1.00
3.	Ed Kessler	Secrets of the Parables 2. Lost and Found and Overpaid	£2.00

Please add postage: 25p plus 10p per £1 over £1.00 order.
Send Cheque payable to Urban Theology Unit.
to UTU, 210 Abbeyfield Rd, Sheffield S4 7AZ